S0-CWR-709

recipes
for KIDS

to lower their
FAT THERMOSTATS

FIRST
EDITION

VITALITY HOUSE INTERNATIONAL, INC.

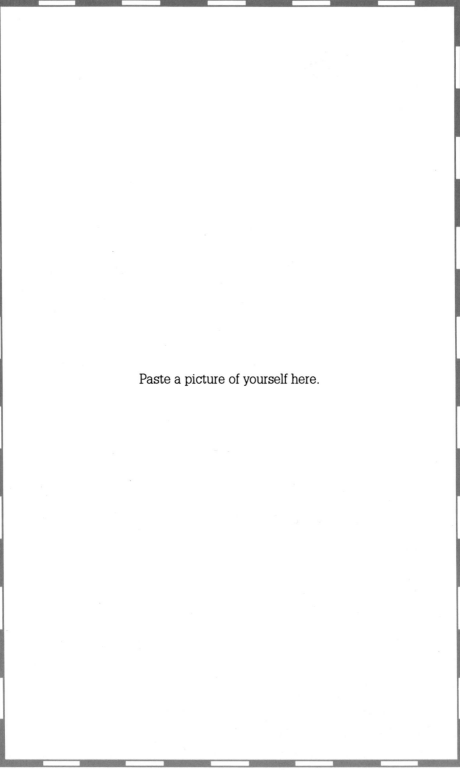

Paste a picture of yourself here.

recipes
for KIDS

to lower their

FAT THERMOSTATS®

FIRST
EDITION

WRITTEN BY
LARENE GAUNT
AND
EDWARD PARENT, PH.D.

ILLUSTRATED BY
RICHARD D. BROWN

INTRODUCTION BY
GARTH FISHER, PH.D.

VITALITY HOUSE INTERNATIONAL, INC.

RECIPES FOR KIDS TO LOWER THEIR FAT THERMOSTATS

Copyright © 1994 by
Vitality House International, Inc.
1675 North Freedom Blvd. #11-C
Provo, Utah 84604

Telephone: 801-373-5100
To order: Call toll-free 1-800-748-5100

First Printing, First Edition, July 1994

All rights reserved. This book or any part thereof may not be reproduced in any form whatsoever without the prior written permission of Vitality House International except in the case of passages used in critical reviews or articles.

This cookbook is a collection of recipes that have been gathered from various sources. All recipes have been adapted to meet a low-fat, low-sugar, low-sodium criteria.

Library of Congress Catalog Card Number: 93-061785
ISBN 0-912547-14-6
Printed by Publishers Press
Salt Lake City, Utah

Publisher's Cataloging in Publication
(*Prepared by Quality Books Inc.*)

Gaunt, LaRene.
Recipes for KIDS to lower their fat thermostats / written by LaRene Gaunt and Edward Parent ; illustrated by Richard D. Brown ; introduction by Garth Fisher. -- 1st ed.
p. cm.
Includes bibliographical references and index.
ISBN 0-912547-14-6

1. Low-fat diet--Recipes--Juvenile literature. 2. Cookery--Juvenile literature. 3. Reducing--Juvenile literature. 4. Low-fat diet--Recipes. 5. Cookery. 6. Weight control. I. Parent, Edward A. II. Title.

RM237.7.G38 1994   641.5'638'
                                    QBI94-1418

To Bethany Parent,
a lively, vivacious ten-year-old,
who cheerfully tested
my recipes and gave me her
honest opinions about them.

To all children and
to the child in each of us.

TABLE OF
CONTENTS

viii Preface
xix About the Authors
x Acknowledgments
xi Introduction

PART 1

1 Lifestyle
5 "Let's Eat"
21 "Let's Play"
25 "Yes, I Can"

PART 2

31 Recipes
32 Nutrition Chart
32 How to Read Labels
34 Like Magic
36 "Sugar and Spice and Everything Nice"
37 "Want to Know a Secret?"
45 "Good Morning"

61 "It's a School Day"
75 "Hooray! It's the Weekend!"
93 "Happy Holidays!"
109 "Can I Cook Dinner Tonight?"

PART 3

123 Tips for Parents
135 Eating Disorders

GAMES

145 The Balancing Act
148 B-A-L-A-N-C-E
149 Tossed Salad
164 The Juggling Act

INDEX

166 Index

PREFACE

Kids,

I hope this book will help you learn how to be the best that you can be. Eating good foods and engaging in lively activities every day will help you look and feel better.

Learning to be happy being "you" is important, too. You have greatness within you, and how you look is only part of what you are. You can do many good things, help others, and be happy right now.

Little by little you can become stronger, healthier, and happier. Every time you pass up junk food, eat fruits and vegetables, or engage in lively activities, you will feel proud of yourself. And you should. This means you are developing self-discipline. That's good!

Choosing to eat nutritious foods and exercise regularly can become good habits. The more you do it, the easier it becomes. Before long, you will be on your way to being an adult with good habits.

I have learned that I feel much better when I follow the guidelines in this book. I know it works. I hope this book will start you on the path to a healthy lifestyle.

I would love to hear from you. Let me know which recipes you like, which ones you don't, and how this program worked for you. If you have any questions, write to:

LaRene Gaunt
c/o Vitality House International, Inc.
1675 North Freedom Blvd. #11-C
Provo, Utah 84604

ABOUT THE AUTHORS
AND ILLUSTRATOR

LaRene Gaunt has worked as an editor for the *Ensign* magazine since 1990. Prior to that, she worked as a freelance writer for ten years and as an accredited genealogist. Born and reared in San Diego, California, LaRene earned a B.A. degree from Brigham Young University in Provo, Utah. After she married, she moved to a small town in Indiana. Living on four acres in a rural setting piqued LaRene's interest in a healthy lifestyle. Jogging down country roads with corn or soybean fields on either side became a habit. Her huge garden overflowed with vegetables, strawberries, and raspberries. Grapes, blueberries, and fruit trees lined the fence rows. Learning to cook and preserve food came as an outgrowth of this experience in nature. LaRene and her husband, David, are the parents of three children.

Edward A. Parent, Ph.D., is a licensed psychologist in private practice. He helps people to cope with the psychological aspects of losing weight, eating disorders, mind-body problems, and abuse. He has recently developed a special interest in helping children who are overweight. Dr. Parent is an admitting physician and consultant to the Eating Disorders Unit and the Depression Unit of Utah Valley Regional Medical Center in Provo, Utah. He is a co-author of *How to Lower Your Fat Thermostat* and *The New Neuropsychology of Weight Control.* A member of several professional societies, Dr. Parent serves as President of Vitality House International, Inc. He and his wife, Sydette, have five children and one grandchild.

Since 1971, Dick Brown has been art director, senior designer, and illustrator for *The Friend*, a children's magazine. Born in Provo, Utah, he studied painting and design at Brigham Young University and graduated with a M.F.A. degree. He was the art director of BYU Graphics for nine years, then creative director for Concepts, Inc., in Salt Lake City, Utah. He has a keen interest in watercolor painting and has exhibited his work in many galleries and shows. Dick has illustrated numerous books and editorial publications over the past thirty years. He particularly enjoys illustrating children's publications. For a bit of diversity, he enjoys golfing and fly fishing. Dick and his wife, June, have five children and five grandchildren.

ACKNOWLEDGMENTS

To Randall White,
whose computer skills helped put this text into
the correct font size, type face, and format.

To Judith M. Paller,
for her precise and careful work in copy
editing and proofreading this cookbook.

To John Luke,
for his superior photography.

To Amy Brown,
for her careful and accurate paste-up.

To Kerry Lynn Herrin,
for her computer skills in setting up the cover,
setting titles, and other invaluable details.

To Mark Robison,
for his valuable service as courier between
authors, illustrator, and typesetter.

To Dennis Remington, M.D., Garth Fisher, Ph.D.,
and Edward Parent, Ph.D., for their outstanding
research and for their book, *How to Lower Your Fat
Thermostat,* which has changed so many lives.

INTRODUCTION

Parents,

Research suggests that weight control is much more complex than simply eating less food. Many thin people eat a lot of food and yet remain thin, while many fat people routinely eat very little and remain fat. The problem is how fat storage is regulated. Thin people regulate their fat storage (weight) at a low level, and overweight people regulate their weight at a higher level. All of us have within our brains control mechanisms that regulate many body functions, including body temperature and storage of body fat. We have called the brain center that controls weight the fat thermostat. Just as the thermostat in our homes keeps the room temperature at the level where it is set (setpoint), the fat thermostat tries to keep our body fat at its setpoint level. The key to successful weight management is to understand which factors influence the setpoint of the fat thermostat, to stop doing those things that keep it too high, and to start doing those things that will lower it.

The fat thermostat is a mechanism we have inherited from our ancestors who survived various famines. It is like a powerful computer that analyzes all the information coming from many sensors within the body. It chooses the body weight that seems appropriate for our needs and works hard to keep it at that level. The weight level selected is a balance between fat and mobility. The body needs enough stored energy to be protected from starvation, and it needs to be mobile enough to run, fight, or migrate if those actions are required.

The fat thermostat works by controlling satiety (feeling full) and hunger. Notice in Diagram 1 that the setpoint is shown at about the level at which the body attains satiety. The stored energy, fat (with a little glycogen), reaches the setpoint level and there is no further signal to eat. As time passes, the body uses energy through physical activities and basal metabolism. The sensors in the body tell the brain that the level of stored energy is falling. When the level of stored energy is low, the brain starts to create signals of physical hunger, which lead to eating. The food eaten replenishes the energy lost, and hunger subsides and is replaced by satiety.

The setpoint is not fixed at one level, as many people believe, but can move up and down. Its initial level is established by the genes. Thereafter it is adjusted by a complex series of feedback loops. Those of our ancestors who had more fat stored had a better chance of surviving a famine. Stress, particularly starvation, raises the setpoint. When an animal is starved it loses weight, mostly fat and muscle. Starvation

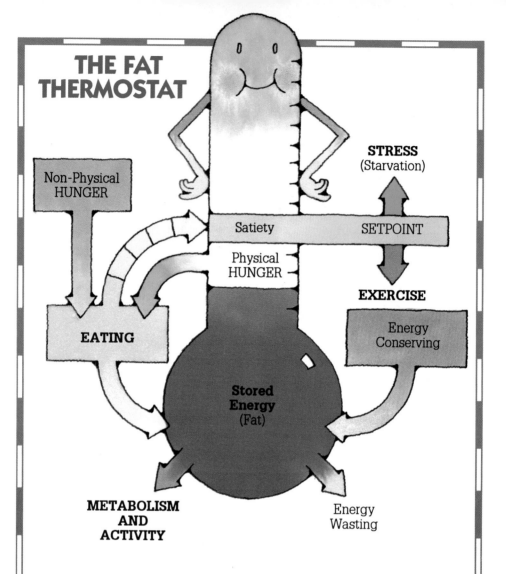

THE FAT THERMOSTAT

Non-Physical HUNGER

STRESS (Starvation)

Satiety   SETPOINT

Physical HUNGER

EXERCISE

EATING

Energy Conserving

Stored Energy (Fat)

METABOLISM AND ACTIVITY

Energy Wasting

causes its setpoint to go up. When the animal can eat again, it more than refills its fat stores. Furthermore, it regains the lost fat faster each time it is forced to starve. As the setpoint goes up, the animal's metabolism slows down. Its energy wasting systems decrease and the energy conserving systems increase. The animal now survives on fewer calories than before.

In addition to starvation dieting,

high-fat and high-sugar foods raise the setpoint. Perhaps the body, fearing another famine, anticipates the need to hold on to as much energy as it can. Of course, the high-fat and high-sugar foods add to the stored energy of the body. If your child eats nutritious foods and does not diet, the fat thermostat can be maintained at an appropriate, lifelong level.

Some of the things besides dieting, fats, and sugars that

increase the setpoint are pregnancy and certain medications and hormones. In addition, there are nonphysical hunger signals that cause us to eat. These include using food to escape an unpleasant task such as homework, using food to celebrate, using food for pleasure, or simply eating out of habit. Some people have no experience with real hunger because they habitually eat; this raises their energy stores above the setpoint level and prevents the body from giving its normal hunger signals. A wide variety of emotions can also trigger nonphysical hunger. These include anxiety, fear, loneliness, boredom, anger, sexual feelings, pain, and even memories of past traumas.

Aerobic exercise tends to move the setpoint downward. Since it is easier to move a lean body, the fat thermostat responds by requiring less stored energy, and excess fat is lost.

Here are the main guidelines that, when followed, should lower your child's fat thermostat for permanent, comfortable weight loss.

1. Eat a wide variety of wholesome food on a regular basis. By providing the body with its complete requirements for calories, vitamins, minerals, and other essential nutrients on a regular basis, the starvation defenses stop being stimulated.

2. Eat in harmony with the hunger drives from the fat thermostat. When we are hungry, we should eat until completely satisfied. Snacking is

not only acceptable, but even encouraged in response to the physical hunger drive. We should eat at least three times daily, and more often if needed.

3. Decrease the consumption of fats. Dietary fats contain more than twice as many calories as carbohydrates and not only raise the fat thermostat, but tend to be stored more efficiently than complex carbohydrates such as vegetables, grains, and fruits. Children are allowed more fats because they are still growing. Adults should keep their fat intake at 20 percent; between 15 and 25 percent of a child's calories can be in the form of fat. Keep in mind that restricting fat intake too strictly is also unhealthy. Certain essential fatty acids and vitamins can be obtained in no other way than through fat-containing foods. Be careful not to restrict fat intake below 15 percent.

4. Reduce sugar intake. Experiments have shown that adding refined sugar to the diet of animals causes them to gain about 50 percent more fat than animals eating the same number of calories but with no sugar. In our society, the average person consumes about 126 pounds of sugar per year. This appears to be a major factor in causing obesity, particularly in children.

5. Exercise effectively. Most overweight children do not enjoy exercise; however, with adequate eating, your child should soon learn to enjoy it. Exercise actually plays several major roles:

a. Exercise lowers the fat

thermostat. Animals in the wild are lean; when caged, they get fat.

b. Exercise helps maintain lean body mass (muscle). Since fat is burned primarily in muscle, muscle loss hurts our efforts to lower fat.

c. Exercise helps change muscle enzyme systems so that they burn fat more effectively.

d. Exercise has been shown to make people feel better. They have more energy and are less depressed. Begin an activity program to set a good example for your child. It does feel good to exercise!

We should follow these common-sense guidelines:

a. Use large muscles in a rhythmic activity such as walking, jogging, riding an exercise bike, aerobic dancing, or swimming.

b. Do these activities at a moderate rate. It should be vigorous enough to increase breathing, but not so hard that you feel breathless or cannot carry on a conversation.

c. We should also exercise daily, starting at about 20 minutes a day and working up to 45 to 60 minutes. We shouldn't increase the exercise time too rapidly. Shorter, more frequent exercise is an effective way to begin without injury.

Be creative with your child to make the activity time more play than work. We should have fun together as we lower our fat thermostats through physical activity.

6. Help reduce stress. Stress seems to raise the setpoint and produce other undesirable biological changes. Carefully listen to your child and attempt to understand his or her feelings. Acknowledge the fear and be careful not to tell your child that it is stupid or unreasonable. By validating your child's concern, he or she can share more feelings with you and probably will find his or her own fear less troublesome.

7. Drink water to satisfy thirst. Water is essential for life. We have a built-in thirst mechanism to tell us when we need water. If we answer our thirst drive by drinking soda pop, alcohol, juice, milk, or other calorie-containing fluids, we are getting unnecessary calories.

In addition, it is very important to distinguish between hunger and thirst. If we are hungry, we need to eat nutritious food which contains fiber, vitamins, and minerals and which provides some chewing and eating satisfaction. If we are thirsty, we need to drink water to satisfy that need. An exception to this general rule is to drink two glasses of skim or low-fat milk.

By following these guidelines, we can help our children lower their fat thermostats and develop habits that can lead to a healthy lifestyle.

A. Garth Fisher, Ph.D.
Director, Human Performance Laboratory,
Brigham Young University, Provo, Utah
Former member of the Council on Health Promotion and Disease Prevention,
U.S. Department of Health and Human Services

LIFESTYLE

PART 1

WHAT IS LIFESTYLE?

The word *lifestyle* refers to how you live your life. In this book, for example, *lifestyle* refers to three important details in your life—food, lively physical activity, and attitude. Each of these three lifestyle details plays an important part in how you look and feel.

In Part 1, we talk about each of these three lifestyle details. In "Let's Eat," we talk about food. In "Let's Play," we talk about lively physical activity. And in "Yes, I Can," we talk about a positive attitude and good self-esteem. We have some control over each of these important parts of our lifestyle.

DOES DIETING WORK?

No. In the past, many people believed that dieting or eating very little would help them become thin and feel good. But dieting never seemed to work. Diets caused people to feel tired and crabby while they lost weight. Dieters always seemed to gain back the weight they had lost.

Now, most people realize that weight control is more complex than simply eating less food. We all know thin people who eat lots of food and yet remain thin. We also know overweight people who eat very little and remain overweight. Why?

Because each of us has within our brain a control mechanism that regulates many body functions, including the storage of fat. This mechanism is called our fat thermostat.

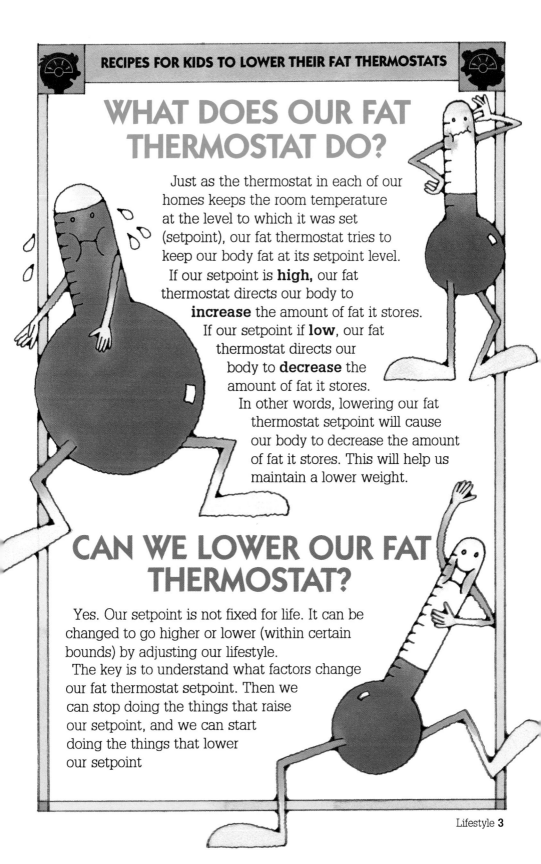

WHAT DOES OUR FAT THERMOSTAT DO?

Just as the thermostat in each of our homes keeps the room temperature at the level to which it was set (setpoint), our fat thermostat tries to keep our body fat at its setpoint level.

If our setpoint is **high,** our fat thermostat directs our body to **increase** the amount of fat it stores. If our setpoint if **low**, our fat thermostat directs our body to **decrease** the amount of fat it stores.

In other words, lowering our fat thermostat setpoint will cause our body to decrease the amount of fat it stores. This will help us maintain a lower weight.

CAN WE LOWER OUR FAT THERMOSTAT?

Yes. Our setpoint is not fixed for life. It can be changed to go higher or lower (within certain bounds) by adjusting our lifestyle.

The key is to understand what factors change our fat thermostat setpoint. Then we can stop doing the things that raise our setpoint, and we can start doing the things that lower our setpoint

HOW
CAN WE LOWER OUR FAT THERMOSTAT?

Making the following adjustments in our lifestyle will allow us to lower our setpoint as much as is healthy and possible for our body. Change comes gradually but permanently. Remember, this is a lifestyle change. It is something we do for the rest of our life, not just for a few months.

1. We need to eat a wide variety of wholesome foods on a regular basis. We don't need to diet. (See "Let's Eat," pp. 5-20.)

2. We need to learn to eat in harmony with our natural hunger drives. In other words: if you are hungry, eat; if you are full, stop eating; and if you are not hungry, don't eat. (See "I'm Hungry," p. 8.)

3. We need to eat less fat, especially saturated (animal) fat. (See "Fats Make Me Fat," pp. 16-19.)

4. We need to eat less sugar and refined foods. (See "Foods for Energy"—Refined [Simple] carbohydrates, p. 10.)

5. We need to engage in lively physical activity. (See "Let's Play," pp. 21-24.)

6. We need to learn to have a positive attitude and good self-esteem. This happens when we learn to focus on the good things that we have in our life instead of focusing on the bad things. (See "Yes, I Can," pp. 25-30.)

"LET'S EAT"

"LET'S EAT"

1. We can categorize the nutritious food we eat into 6 main categories:

Complex CARBOHYDRATES (pp. 10-11)

FRUITS (p. 12)

VEGETABLES (p. 13)

PROTEIN (pp. 14-15)

Unsaturated FATS (pp. 16-19)

Low-Fat DAIRY (p. 20)

2. Our goal is to eat a variety of foods that are low in fat and high in complex carbohydrates. This combination should result in foods that are high in fiber and low in cholesterol, and that provide adequate protein.

3. Most of the time, grains, pasta, or beans should form the basis of what we eat. Meat can be added in small amounts to these items. Vegetables and fruits can round out the rest of our meal.

4. Sometimes, meat can be the main course. When it is, eat fish or chicken or other low-fat meats in small portions.

5. We should eat fats and sugars sparingly.

6. We should eat only when we are hungry.

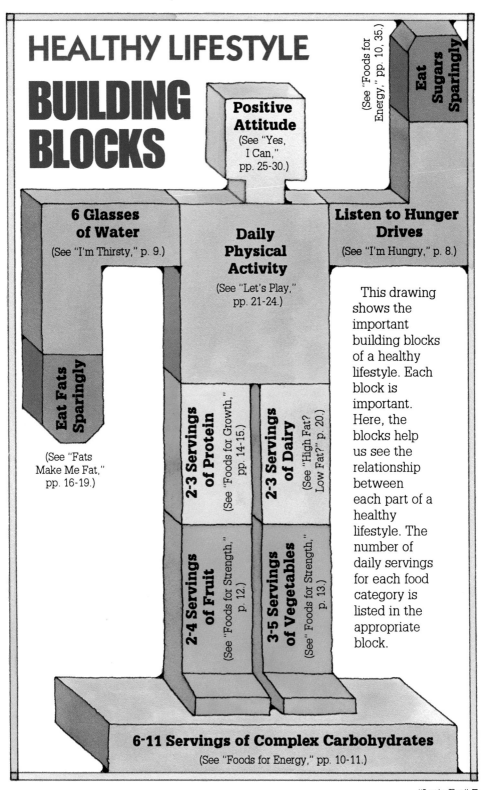

HEALTHY LIFESTYLE
BUILDING BLOCKS

Positive Attitude
(See "Yes, I Can," pp. 25-30.)

Eat Sugars Sparingly
(See "Foods for Energy," pp. 10, 35.)

6 Glasses of Water
(See "I'm Thirsty," p. 9.)

Daily Physical Activity
(See "Let's Play," pp. 21-24.)

Listen to Hunger Drives
(See "I'm Hungry," p. 8.)

Eat Fats Sparingly
(See "Fats Make Me Fat," pp. 16-19.)

2-3 Servings of Protein
(See "Foods for Growth," pp. 14-15.)

2-3 Servings of Dairy
(See "High Fat? Low Fat?" p. 20.)

2-4 Servings of Fruit
(See "Foods for Strength," p. 12.)

3-5 Servings of Vegetables
(See "Foods for Strength," p. 13.)

This drawing shows the important building blocks of a healthy lifestyle. Each block is important. Here, the blocks help us see the relationship between each part of a healthy lifestyle. The number of daily servings for each food category is listed in the appropriate block.

6-11 Servings of Complex Carbohydrates
(See "Foods for Energy," pp. 10-11.)

"I'M HUNGRY"

1. Our bodies will let us know when we need to eat. We will feel hungry, and we will have fun learning to recognize that feeling. We should eat regularly, at least 3 times a day, and snack at other times if we are hungry.

2. Don't confuse hunger drives with thirst. When we are hungry between meals, we should drink a glass of water and wait 10 minutes. If we are still hungry, we should eat food that requires lots of chewing.

Remember, it takes about 20 minutes for your stomach to tell your brain that you are full. So, eat slowly. Don't eat when you feel full. If you do, 20 minutes later you might get a stomachache.

SERVING SIZES

We should eat at least the suggested number of servings from each food category each day.

Complex CARBOHYDRATES (6-11 servings):
1 slice of bread
1/2 cup of cereal, rice, or pasta

FRUIT (2-4 servings):
1/2 cup chopped fruit
3/4 cup fruit juice
1 medium orange, apple, or banana

VEGETABLES (3-5 servings):
1 cup raw leafy vegetables
1/2 cup cooked or raw vegetables
3/4 cup vegetable juice

PROTEIN (2-3 servings):
1/2 cup cooked beans
1 egg
2 ounces cooked meat (lean beef, poultry, fish)
1 ounce cooked meat (not lean)
2 tablespoons peanut butter

FATS and SUGARS (sparingly):
1 teaspoon oil, mayonnaise, butter, or margarine

Low-fat DAIRY (2-3 servings):
1 cup skim or 1% milk
1 1/2 ounces cheese
1 cup plain yogurt

"I'M THIRSTY"

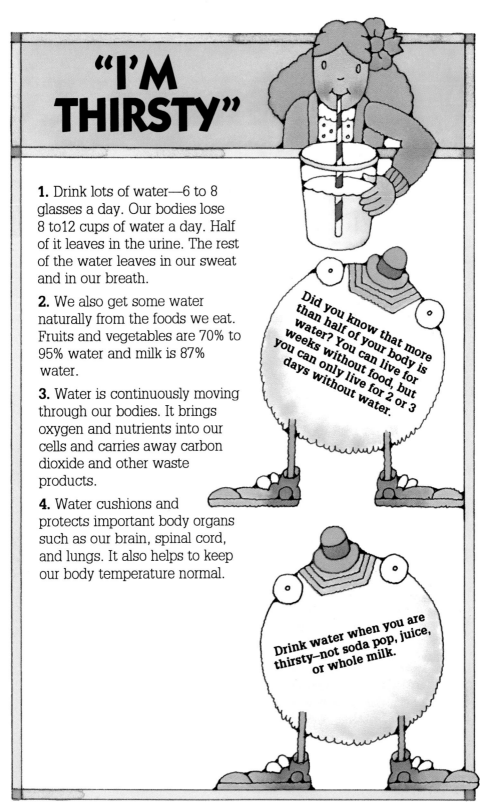

1. Drink lots of water—6 to 8 glasses a day. Our bodies lose 8 to12 cups of water a day. Half of it leaves in the urine. The rest of the water leaves in our sweat and in our breath.

2. We also get some water naturally from the foods we eat. Fruits and vegetables are 70% to 95% water and milk is 87% water.

3. Water is continuously moving through our bodies. It brings oxygen and nutrients into our cells and carries away carbon dioxide and other waste products.

4. Water cushions and protects important body organs such as our brain, spinal cord, and lungs. It also helps to keep our body temperature normal.

Did you know that more than half of your body is water? You can live for weeks without food, but you can only live for 2 or 3 days without water.

Drink water when you are thirsty—not soda pop, juice, or whole milk.

CARBOHYDRATES
REFINED
(SIMPLE)

The best parts of me are missing!

Refined carbohydrates are loaded with calories but have little food value.

Eating sugar greatly increases our chances of getting cavities.

There are two kinds of carbohydrates: refined and unrefined. Refined carbohydrates are also called simple carbohydrates because they have only a few molecules in them. They break down quickly in our digestive system. As they break down, there is a sharp increase of glucose (sugar) in our bloodstream, followed by a sharp increase in insulin, followed by a sharp drop in glucose.

Unrefined carbohydrates are also called complex carbohydrates because they have many molecules in them. They break down slowly in our digestive system. As they break down, there is a gradual increase of glucose followed by a gradual increase of insulin.

Endosperm (starch)

REFINED WHOLE WHEAT

Some foods high in refined carbohydrates:

sugar = white, raw, brown

*Also high in fat

pie*

white rice

white flour

maple syrup

molasses

corn syrup

cake*

honey

donuts*

cookies*

CARBOHYDRATES
UNREFINED
(COMPLEX)

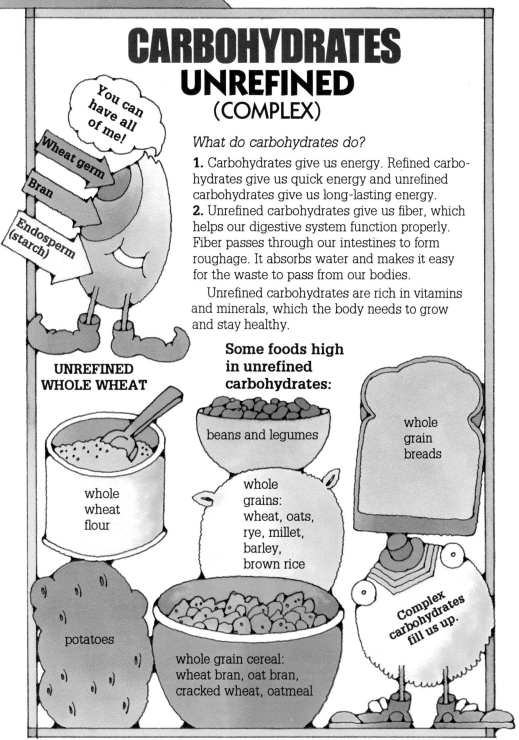

You can have all of me!

Wheat germ

Bran

Endosperm (starch)

UNREFINED WHOLE WHEAT

What do carbohydrates do?

1. Carbohydrates give us energy. Refined carbo-hydrates give us quick energy and unrefined carbohydrates give us long-lasting energy.

2. Unrefined carbohydrates give us fiber, which helps our digestive system function properly. Fiber passes through our intestines to form roughage. It absorbs water and makes it easy for the waste to pass from our bodies.

Unrefined carbohydrates are rich in vitamins and minerals, which the body needs to grow and stay healthy.

Some foods high in unrefined carbohydrates:

beans and legumes

whole grain breads

whole wheat flour

whole grains: wheat, oats, rye, millet, barley, brown rice

potatoes

whole grain cereal: wheat bran, oat bran, cracked wheat, oatmeal

Complex carbohydrates fill us up.

watermelon

FRUITS

What do vitamins and minerals do?

1. Vitamins and minerals are the builders of our bodies. Minerals help build teeth and bones. Vitamins and minerals build blood cells, body tissue, skin, and eyes.

2. Vitamins help our bodies fight germs and diseases.

3. Vitamins are made by plants—fruits, vegetables, and grains.

4. Minerals are in all foods.

Fruits have a natural sweetness.

Berries, plums, pears, apples, cherries, and bananas are especially high in fiber.

Eat sparingly: olives (89% fat); avocados (82% fat).

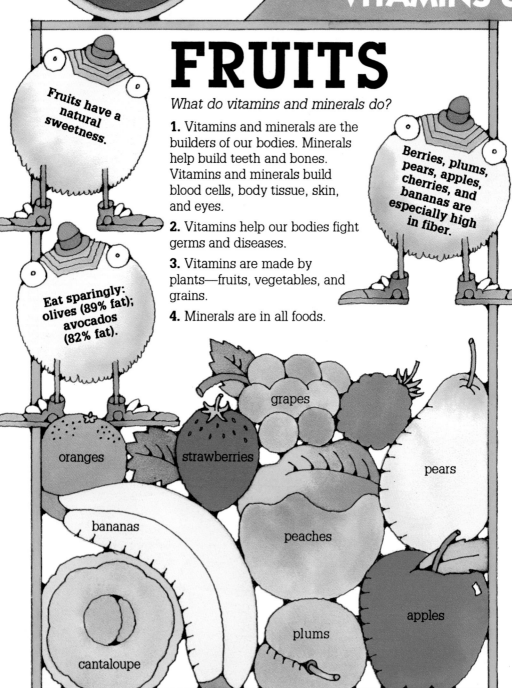

grapes

oranges

strawberries

pears

bananas

peaches

cantaloupe

plums

apples

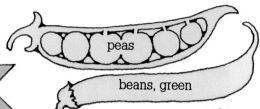

peas

beans, green

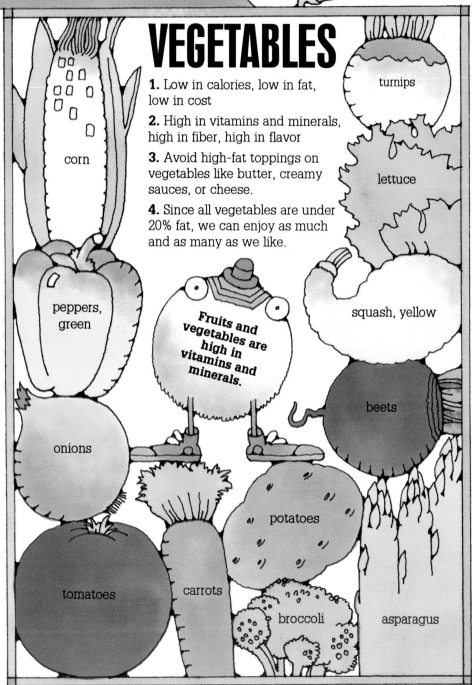

VEGETABLES

1. Low in calories, low in fat, low in cost

2. High in vitamins and minerals, high in fiber, high in flavor

3. Avoid high-fat toppings on vegetables like butter, creamy sauces, or cheese.

4. Since all vegetables are under 20% fat, we can enjoy as much and as many as we like.

corn

turnips

lettuce

peppers, green

Fruits and vegetables are high in vitamins and minerals.

squash, yellow

onions

beets

potatoes

tomatoes

carrots

broccoli

asparagus

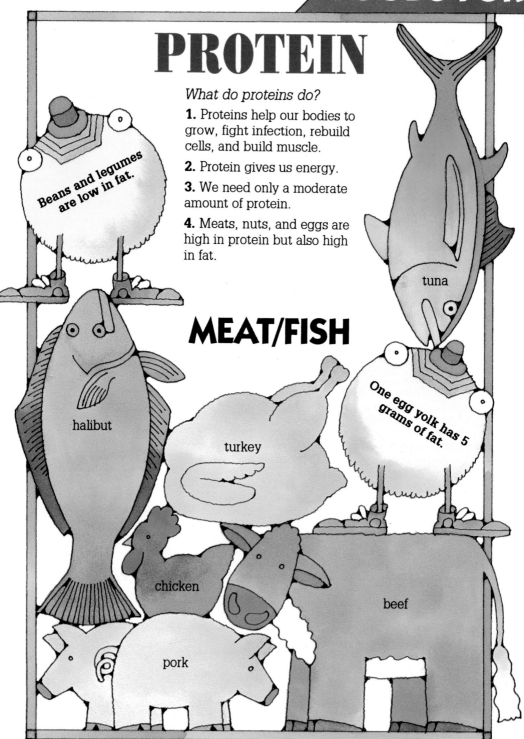

PROTEIN

What do proteins do?

1. Proteins help our bodies to grow, fight infection, rebuild cells, and build muscle.

2. Protein gives us energy.

3. We need only a moderate amount of protein.

4. Meats, nuts, and eggs are high in protein but also high in fat.

MEAT/FISH

Beans and legumes are low in fat.

tuna

halibut

turkey

One egg yolk has 5 grams of fat.

chicken

beef

pork

BEANS/LEGUMES

Beans (kidney, red, white, pinto) and legumes (peas, split peas, and lentils) are filled with protein and fiber but have very little fat. They are filling.

red beans

peas

pinto beans

Beans and legumes are high in protein and complex carbohydrates.

white beans

kidney beans

peanuts
(high in fat)

split peas

Nuts and eggs are high in protein but both are also high in fat.

low-fat refried beans

chili

FATS MAKE

Cholesterol is found only in animal fat.

Fat comes in 2 types: saturated (from animals) and unsaturated (from plants).

What do fats do?

1. Store energy

2. Dissolve fat-soluble vitamins

Cholesterol can collect in our veins and arteries.

eggs

SATURATED
FAT

Some foods high in unsaturated fat:

butter or margarine

mayonnaise

cream or whole milk

pork

cheese

beef

Beware of palm oil and coconut oil!

shortening or lard

UNSATURATED
FAT

There is no cholesterol in unsaturated fats.

Some foods high in unsaturated fat:

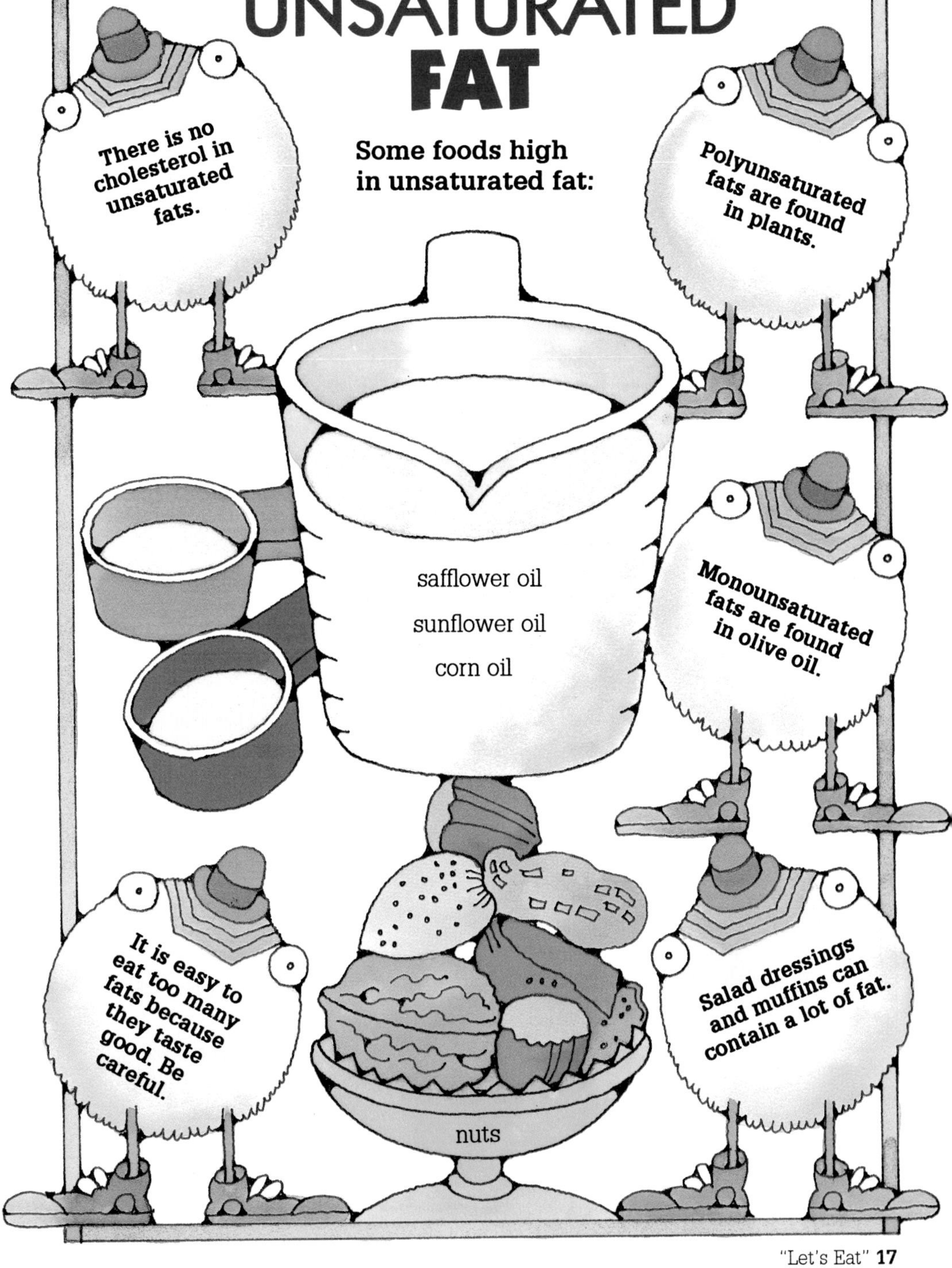

Polyunsaturated fats are found in plants.

safflower oil

sunflower oil

corn oil

Monounsaturated fats are found in olive oil.

It is easy to eat too many fats because they taste good. Be careful.

nuts

Salad dressings and muffins can contain a lot of fat.

What is a calorie?
A *calorie* is the unit for measuring the energy released when food is oxidized in our muscles.

Our goal is to help our bodies become efficient at burning calories in the same way a furnace can become efficient at burning wood for heat.

Regular physical activity, nutritious foods, and a positive attitude can lower our fat thermostat and make our body efficient at burning calories. As we burn our fat supply, we will feel additional energy.

Being a couch potato, eating junk food, and having a negative attitude can raise our fat thermostat and make our bodies ineffective at burning calories. We will feel sluggish and maintain our fat supply.

There are 3,500 calories in one pound of fat.

COUNTING GRAMS OF FAT INSTEAD OF CALORIES

Nutrition is more important than calories. Count the grams of fat instead of calories. Why? Because fats have more than twice as many calories per gram than protein or carbohydrates.

1 gram protein = 4 calories
1 gram carbohydrate = 4 calories
1 gram fat = 9 calories

Counting the grams of fat will also help us learn which foods are high in fat and help us to become aware of serving sizes.
We can:
1. Keep a running total of the grams of fat we eat each day. Children can eat more fat than adults. About 25% of a child's daily calories can come from fat. The grams of fat are listed with each recipe in this book. They are in the chart at the bottom of each recipe

under the letter "F." (See p. 32.)
2. Or we can make sure everything we eat is under 25% fat. The percentage of fat is listed with each recipe in this book. It is in the chart at the bottom of each recipe under "%Fat." (See p. 32 for more information.)
The following table can help you with other foods that you eat. Read the label and allow 3 grams of fat per 100 calories.

TABLE

100 calories = 3 grams or less
200 calories = 6 grams or less
300 calories = 9 grams or less

HIGH-FAT? LOW-FAT?

DAIRY

What about dairy foods?

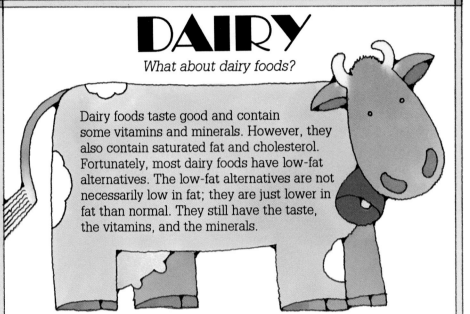

Dairy foods taste good and contain some vitamins and minerals. However, they also contain saturated fat and cholesterol. Fortunately, most dairy foods have low-fat alternatives. The low-fat alternatives are not necessarily low in fat; they are just lower in fat than normal. They still have the taste, the vitamins, and the minerals.

Some high-fat dairy foods and their low-fat alternatives:

HIGH-FAT

1. Cheese from whole milk
2. Cream, whole milk
3. Whole eggs or egg yolks
4. Yogurt made from whole milk
5. Ice cream

LOW-FAT

1. Cheese from skim milk
2. Skim milk, buttermilk, 1% milk, 2% milk
3. Egg whites
4. Yogurt made from skim or 1% milk
5. Ice milk or sherbet

"LET'S PLAY"

SEVERAL TIMES A DAY–
PLAY!

Play with a friend and have twice the fun!

The best thing you can do for yourself is to play every day. Play anything you want, whenever you want, as often as you want, but keep moving.

Use the large muscles in your arms and legs again and again.

WHY KEEP MOVING?

1. Playing makes you feel happy. Your brain releases chemicals called endorphins when you exercise. Endorphins make you feel good.

2. Playing lowers your fat thermostat. Sitting around like a couch potato raises your fat thermostat.

3. Playing helps your body build strong muscles. Muscles are important because you burn fat in them.

4. With lots of regular exercise, your body will become more efficient at burning fat.

5. Playing is fun!

"YES, I CAN"

"I'M OKAY"

Some kids are tall and some are short; some have black hair and some have blond hair. We all look a little bit different, and that's good. It would be boring if we all looked alike.

One of the ways in which we are different is in our body type. We each are more or less one of three body types.

1
Some kids are skinny and angular. Their body type is called ectomorphic.

2
Other kids are more rounded. Their body type is called endomorphic.

3
And still other kids are muscular and solid. Their body type is called mesomorphic.

No one body type is right; they are all okay. They are just different. Which body type are you? Once you know, you will understand why you look the way you do. Then it will be easier for you to look the best you can for your body type.

Don't compare yourself to others. Just be you. And remember, you're okay!

"I'M IN CHARGE!"

We have more control over what we do, what we eat, and how we feel than we may realize.

For example, sometimes we feel unhappy because things don't go the way we want them to go. We may feel like one of these kids:

Billy has red hair. Some kids tease him because of his hair color and freckles. "I get mad," he says, "and I feel like hitting them."

BILLY

Betty says, "I hate playing sports. When the kids choose teams at school, I'm usually the last one picked. I feel like crying."

John tries as hard as he can to understand long division. "I try but I still get bad grades," he says. "I wish I didn't have to take math."

BETTY

Do you ever feel like this? Most of us do once in a while. Times like these are stressful. Too much stress can raise our fat thermostat.

Believe it or not, we are in charge of how we feel. When others say or do

JOHN

mean things to us, it might hurt at first, but we can learn to control how long mean things will hurt us. We don't have to let our feelings be hurt. We can ignore bad things and think of good things instead. If we have a good sense of humor, we can even make a joke about bad things.

What we think about ourselves is more important than what others think of us. Always remember, we have greatness within us. Knowing we are valuable helps us feel better about ourselves and reduces our stress. That helps lower our fat thermostat.

Another way we help ourselves be happy is to learn self-control. Self-control means that we develop good habits. As we learn good habits, our bad habits disappear. This is easier to do when others around us are trying to learn the same good habits. However, if we need to, we can do it on our own.

SOCIAL PRESSURE

What do we do when we are with people who like to eat junk food? If we are with a friend, we can suggest eating something else. If we are with others, we can move away from the food, chew gum, or drink a glass of water. We can do these things quietly.

LOCATION

What do we do when we want junk foods when we watch television, a movie, or a sports event? What do we do when there is junk food at a friend's house? Any change that will keep us from eating junk food is okay. Turn off the television or do something with your hands, like coloring, while you watch television. When possible eat a low-fat snack. Raw vegetables are good. So are fruit juice popsicles.

TIME OF DAY

What do we do when we want to eat junk foods at certain times of the day, such as when we get home from school or just before bedtime? If possible, change the pattern of your day. For example, walk the dog after school instead of eating, or read a book before you go to bed.

Otherwise, replace junk foods with nutritious foods.

LIFE
STYLE
CHART

We may do some things or eat some things out of habit. Habits are part of our lifestyle. In order to be in control of our lifestyle, we need to see if we have any habits that negatively influence our actions. Use the following chart to help you understand your lifestyle. See pp. 164-65 for more ideas.

Time	What did I eat?	Why?	Where?	With whom?

RECIPES

PART 2

NUTRITION CHART

At the bottom of each recipe is a chart. This chart contains important nutritional information about each recipe. ("T" means trace.)

Cal = calories per serving

%Ft = percent of fat per serving

P = grams of protein per serving

F = grams of fat per serving

C = grams of carbohydrate per serving

	Cal	%Ft	P	F	C
Per Pizza	263	24	18	7	37

HOW TO READ LABELS

Labels appear on packaged foods in the grocery store. They usually have a nutrition chart on the side or the back of the package that contains the same important information as the chart above. The words *Nutrition Facts* usually appear at the top of these charts.

You should learn to read these charts so you will know exactly what you are eating. A typical chart looks like this:

NUTRITION FACTS

Serving Size = amount considered to be 1 serving.

Servings per Container = number of servings in the box or can.

Calories = number of calories in the serving size.

Calories from fat = calories per serving from fat.

% Daily Value = percentages are based on a 2,000 calorie daily diet.

Total Fat = grams of fat in the serving size.

Saturated Fat = grams of saturated fat in the serving size. (Saturated fat is from animal products such as meat, milk, or eggs. Unsaturated fat is from plant products such as corn or olives.)

Cholesterol = milligrams of cholesterol per serving size.

Sodium = milligrams of salt per serving size.

Total Carbohydrates = total grams of unrefined (complex) carbohydrates and refined (simple) carbohydrates per serving size.

Dietary Fiber = grams of fiber in the serving size. (Fiber is left in your digestive system after your body digests complex carbohydrates. It is important in helping your digestive system work correctly.)

Sugars = grams of refined (simple) carbohydrates per serving size.

Protein = grams of protein per serving size.

A list of vitamins and minerals usually follows the chart of Nutrition Facts—Vitamin A, Vitamin C, calcium, and iron are required to be listed. Larger packages may have a section that tells the number of calories per gram of fat, carbohydrate, and protein. It is always: Fat 9; Carbohydrate 4; and Protein 4. (See p. 19.)

Ingredients

A list of ingredients usually follows the list of vitamins and minerals. These ingredients are always listed in order from the most to the least.

JUNK FOODS

Once you learn how to read labels, you can choose foods with high nutritional value. Foods with little nutritional value but lots of fat or sugar are called "junk foods." They contain mostly calories.

Candy and some dry cereals are examples of foods that are mostly sugar.

Cookies, ice cream, cake, and pie are examples of foods that are high in both sugar and fat.

Potato chips and French fries are examples of foods that are high in fat.

LESS FAT

Are some of your favorite foods too high in fat? You can change them like magic—it's easy!

1. Replace 1 whole egg with 2 egg whites.

2. Replace whole milk with skim milk or 1% milk.

3. Replace sour cream with plain yogurt.

4. Replace oil-packed tuna with water-packed tuna.

5. Replace butter with low-fat spread, Butter Buds®, or Molly McButter®.

6. Make creamy salad dressing with 1 cup plain yogurt and 1 tablespoon ranch dressing.

7. Replace beef with chicken.

8. Replace mayonnaise or butter with mustard or barbecue sauce.

MAGIC

LESS SUGAR

Got a sweet tooth? Here are some ideas for you.

1. Replace sugar with frozen fruit juice concentrate. Use the same amount.

2. Replace sugar with honey. Use half as much honey as sugar (honey is twice as sweet as sugar).

3. Eat canned fruit packed in its own juice instead of in heavy syrup.

4. Top pancakes with applesauce instead of maple syrup.

5. Learn to use spices and extracts for flavor instead of sugar.

6. Eat high-fat or high-sugar foods less often. When you eat them, eat only half as much as you would normally.

7. Drink a glass of water instead of eating.

"SUGAR & SPICE AND EVERYTHING NICE"

Everyone likes their food to taste good. Often, sugar, salt, and fat (such as butter) are added to our foods to make them taste stronger. Stronger flavors are not always better flavors.

Since we know it is better for us to eat less sugar, salt, and fat, it is important to do two things:

1. Learn to appreciate the natural flavor of foods. For example, fresh fruits have their own sweet taste. Vegetables are not sweet but have a crunchy texture and allow us to chew and enjoy their flavor for a long time.

2. Learn which seasonings can replace sugar, salt, and fat.

Look at the spices that are in your kitchen. Do this with an adult or get an adult's permission to do it. Take all of the spices, flavorings, and extracts out of the cupboard. Open each one and smell it. You can tell how each tastes by how it smells.

Now, see how many of the spices in your kitchen are on the list below. You do not need everything on the list. Suggest to an adult that you buy some of the spices that you do not have.

SUGAR REPLACEMENTS

Vanilla extract	Allspice	Apple pie spice
Orange extract	Cinnamon	Dried orange peel
Mint extract	Nutmeg	Dried lemon peel
Peppermint extract	Ginger	Cloves, ground or whole
Maple extract	Pumpkin pie spice	Anise

Frozen fruit juice concentrates, such as orange juice or apple juice concentrate, can replace sugar in most recipes.

SALT REPLACEMENTS

Oregano	Sage	Mrs. Dash®	Garlic Powder
Basil	Italian Seasoning	Spike®	Onion powder
Thyme	Lemon and pepper	Minced onions	Chili Powder

FAT REPLACEMENTS

Butter Buds®   Molly McButter®

"WANT TO KNOW A SECRET?"

COOKING SECRETS

Read this chapter. It is filled with secrets that will help you learn how to cook.

Even if you have cooked before, reading this chapter will be a good review of cooking tips, safety tips, cooking tools, cooking terms, and kitchen math.

If you have never cooked before, read this chapter with an adult who can answer your questions. An adult can also show you how to use the stove and where all of the kitchen tools are stored.

Cooking is lots of fun. So read this chapter, then find a recipe on one of the following pages and give it a try. HAPPY EATING!

1. Read the recipe, then check to make sure you have all of the ingredients.

2. Put all of the ingredients and the kitchen tools on the work area before you start to cook.

3. Wash your hands with soap and water. Dry them well.

4. Put on an apron to keep your clothes clean while you cook.

5. Fill the sink with warm, soapy water and put your dirty dishes in it as you cook.

6. When you start cooking, put each ingredient away after you use it.

7. Make sure the kitchen is clean when you are finished. Wipe the work area and the stove top with a damp dishrag.

SAFETY
SECRETS

1. To avoid electrical shock, make sure your hands are dry when you touch the plug or switch on an appliance. Unplug appliances by pulling on the plug; never pull on the cord.

2. Use a cutting board when chopping or slicing vegetables or fruits, so you don't damage the countertop or the knife.

3. Ask an adult for help when using the stove, oven, blender, microwave, or a knife.

4. When using a saucepan on the stove, turn the handle to the side or back so that it does not stick out over the edge of the stove.

5. Keep hotpads and towels away from the stove top. They could catch on fire.

6. When stirring food in a saucepan on the stove, use a long-handled wooden spoon because it will not get hot.

7. Wipe up any spills on the floor immediately so that you do not slip and fall.

8. Use thick pot holders when you take pans off the stove or out of the oven. Be careful! The heat can burn you.

9. Lift the lid of a saucepan away from you so that the steam will not burn your face or hands.

10. Wash knives separately. Be careful of the blades.

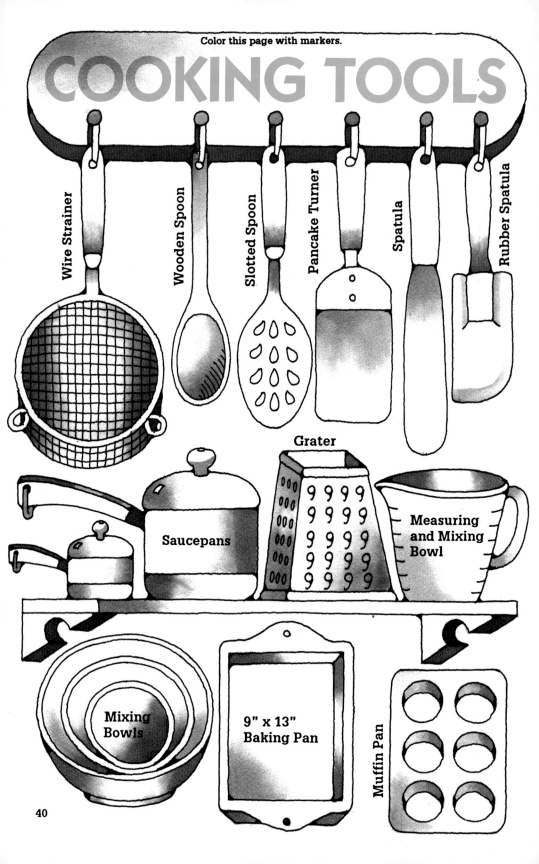

Color this page with markers.

COOKING TOOLS

Wire Strainer

Wooden Spoon

Slotted Spoon

Pancake Turner

Spatula

Rubber Spatula

Grater

Saucepans

Measuring and Mixing Bowl

Mixing Bowls

9" x 13" Baking Pan

Muffin Pan

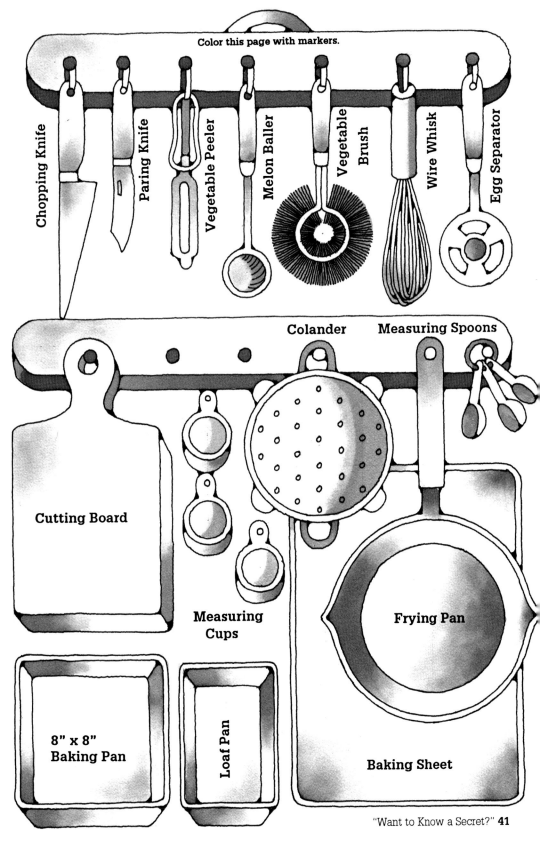

Color this page with markers.

Chopping Knife

Paring Knife

Vegetable Peeler

Melon Baller

Vegetable Brush

Wire Whisk

Egg Separator

Colander

Measuring Spoons

Cutting Board

Measuring Cups

Frying Pan

8" x 8" Baking Pan

Loaf Pan

Baking Sheet

COOKING TERMS

Color this page with markers.

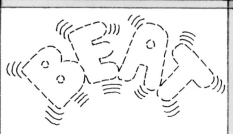

Use a spoon, fork, whisk, eggbeater, or electric mixer to mix ingredients together, using a fast, circular motion.

Rinse fresh fruits and vegetables under running water. To scrub potatoes or carrots, use a vegetable brush or dishrag while holding food under running water.

In this book, the word *blend* refers to using an electric blender. Keep the lid on when running a blender. Use medium speed for a short time.

Use a spoon to mix ingredients together, using a slow, circular motion. Use a long-handled wooden spoon when stirring food on the stove.

Canned fruit needs to be strained. Over a sink or bowl, pour the canned fruit into a strainer. The liquid goes into the bowl or sink and the fruit stays in the strainer.

Cut fruits, vegetables, and meat into small pieces about 1/2-inch square. Use a cutting board and a knife.

Use vegetable cooking spray instead of grease on baking pans or frying pans. This will greatly reduce the amount of fat in your food.

Cheese is often grated. Place a grater over a bowl. Rub a block of cheese against the sharp edge of the grater. It cuts the cheese into small shreds.

To simmer food in a frying pan or saucepan on the stove top, cook it at a low temperature.

To serve food cold, put it in a covered container and leave it in the refrigerator for 2 hours or longer.

To boil water in a saucepan, cook it at a high temperature until bubbles begin to rise rapidly to the surface.

HOW TO MEASURE

1. Measure all ingredients carefully and exactly.

2. Measure dry ingredients, such as flour and sugar, in a measuring cup for dry ingredients. Use the edge of a spatula to level the ingredients even with the top of the measuring cup. Do not pack dry ingredients down, except for brown sugar.

3. Measure liquids, such as water or milk, in a measuring cup for liquids. Set the measuring cup on a level countertop. Bend down so that your eyes are level with the mark on the cup. Pour the liquid into the cup to the desired mark.

4. Measure small amounts of liquids or of dry ingredients in measuring spoons. For liquids, fill the spoon to the top. For dry ingredients, use the edge of a spatula to level the ingredients even with the top of the spoon.

KITCHEN MATH

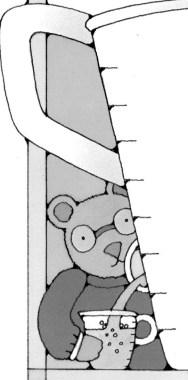

pinch = 1/8 teaspoon
3 teaspoons = 1 tablespoon
4 tablespoons = 1/4 cup
1/4 cup + 1/4 cup = 1/2 cup
1/2 cup + 1/2 cup = 1 cup
1 cup = 8 ounces
2 cups = 1 pint = 16 ounces
2 pints = 1 quart = 32 ounces
2 quarts = 1/2 gallon = 64 ounces
1 pound = 16 ounces

Other abbreviations:
tsp. = teaspoon
Tbl. = tablespoon
pkg. = package
oz. = ounce
med. = medium

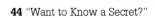

"GOOD MORNING"

ARE YOU A BREAKFAST SKIPPER?

Do you say you aren't hungry in the morning? Or maybe you think that you don't have time to eat before you go to school.

Well, don't skip breakfast anymore! You need it! While you were asleep your body slowed down, and the only way to get it back up to speed again is to eat breakfast.

With so many yummy things to eat for breakfast, you won't need to be a breakfast skipper anymore. Fill up on high-fiber food like cereals, breads, muffins, or pancakes. You will feel full without eating too many calories. Or drink an Alaskan Sunrise (p. 52) on a warm summer morning. Try scrambled eggs (pp. 90, 98) with hash brown potatoes (p. 91) one morning for a change. If you oversleep, take an apple or a banana to eat on the way to school (p. 63).

So what do you say? Give it a try and decide today to become a breakfast eater instead of a breakfast skipper!

OTHER BREAKFAST IDEAS

1 School Bus Breakfasts (p. 63)

2 Funny-Face Sandwich (p. 66)

3 Tutti-Frutti Treat (p. 67)

4 Up and Down the Scales (p. 70)

5 Wiggle, Waggle, Jiggle, Jaggle (pp. 72-73)

6 Ice Hockey (p. 79)

7 Tic-Tac-Toe Fruit Combo (p. 88)

8 Scrambled Surprise (p. 90)

9 Skillet Skitters (p. 91)

10 Ham and Green Eggs (p. 98)

11 Four Seasons of Salads (pp. 100-1)

12 Frozen Fruit Snow (p. 105)

GOING APE

This makes a great breakfast or a snack. You can add fruit, such as grated apples, raisins, crushed pineapple, sliced peaches, mandarin oranges, grapes, applesauce, berries, or melon balls. Or add a spoonful of Jungle Jumble (p. 49).

1/2	cup	rolled oats, quick
1	tsp.	sugar
1/2	cup	milk, skim or 1%
1/2		banana, sliced

Yield: 1 serving

1. In a bowl, mix the rolled oats, sugar, and milk together.

2. Let the mixture sit for a few minutes until the rolled oats absorb some of the milk.

3. Stir in the sliced banana. Eat and enjoy!

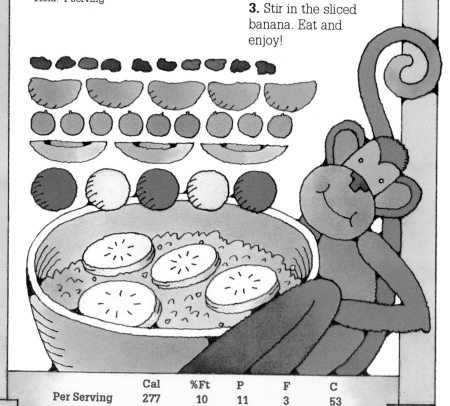

	Cal	%Ft	P	F	C
Per Serving	277	10	11	3	53

JUNGLE JUMBLE

*If you make this
the night before and put it
in the refrigerator, it will be waiting
for you in the morning for a quick breakfast.*

1		20-oz. can pineapple chunks, drained
1	cup	grapes, rinsed
2		bananas, peeled and sliced
1		red apple, chopped
1		orange, cut into bite-sized pieces
1	tsp.	lemon juice

1. Get out a large bowl (one with a tight-fitting lid, if possible). Pour the pineapple chunks and the grapes into the bowl.

2. Add the sliced bananas, chopped apple, and orange pieces.

3. Put the lid on the bowl. Hold on tightly to the bowl and lid and gently tip the bowl upside down and back to "jumble" the fruit. Tip bowl 3 more times. If you don't have a bowl with a lid, just stir the fruit together.

4. Spoon 1 cup of the mixture into a small bowl and enjoy the naturally sweet flavor of fresh fruit.

5. Store leftover Jungle Jumble in the refrigerator in a covered container. It will keep for one or two days.

IDEA: Add a spoonful of Jungle Jumble to Going Ape (p. 48) or to 1/2 cup low-fat vanilla yogurt, or pour over Birthday Banana Split (p. 104).

Yield: 6 (1-cup) servings

	Cal	%Ft	P	F	C
Per Serving	131	2	1	3	32

FROM THE

Maybe you want to eat cold cereal for breakfast. That's okay, but choose a low-fat, low-sugar cold cereal from the following: Shredded Wheat, Cheerios, Puffed Wheat, Puffed Rice, Rice Chex, Corn Chex, Wheat Chex, Grape-Nuts, Rice Krispies, Wheaties, Corn Flakes, Bran Flakes.

There are others, too. Just look on the grocery shelf. But be careful and read the label (see p. 32). Many cold cereals are high in sugar. A suggested limit is 3 grams of sugar per serving.

AIRBORNE

This fluffy, puffy combination also makes a good snack.

1/2 cup	vanilla yogurt, low-fat
3/4 cup	Rice Krispies

1. Pour yogurt in a bowl.

2. Add the Rice Krispies and stir gently. If you like, sprinkle cinnamon on top. Eat immediately and you'll feel as light as air!

IDEA: Replace Rice Krispies with Cheerios, Puffed Rice, or Rice Chex.

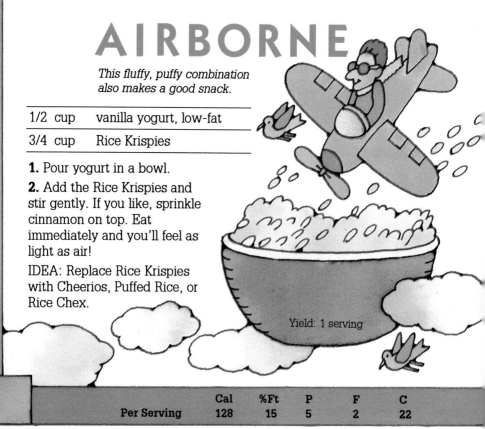

Yield: 1 serving

	Cal	%Ft	P	F	C
Per Serving	128	15	5	2	22

Hot cereal is a great breakfast. Choose from the following list of low-fat, low-sugar hot cereals: Rolled Oats, Malt-O-Meal, Zoom, Wheat Hearts, Oat Bran, Cream of Wheat. Remember, there are others, too. Just read the labels.

GROCERY SHELF

"GO GET DRESSED FOR SCHOOL" OATMEAL

This is yummy with chopped apples, cinnamon, or vanilla extract added to it.

1	cup	water
1/3	cup	rolled oats, quick
1	tsp.	brown sugar
1/4	cup	milk, skim or 1%
1	tsp.	Gifford's Dessert Spice® (p. 178)

1. Do not turn on the stove yet. Combine water and rolled oats in a 2-quart saucepan. Let mixture sit on the kitchen counter for about 10 minutes while you get dressed for school.

2. When you come back, put the saucepan on the stove. Turn the stove on to medium high. Cook until it begins to boil. Stir mixture occasionally. Cook about 1 minute.

3. Turn off the stove. Put a lid on the pan. Remove the pan from the stove. Let it set while you get a bowl and spoon.

4. Scoop the oatmeal into a bowl. Top it with brown sugar and milk. What a nice warm way to start your day! (But be careful and don't spill any on your school clothes.)

Yield: 1 serving

	Cal	%Ft	P	F	C
Per Serving	142	12	6	2	26

ALASKAN SUNRISE

Milk can be frozen in an ice cube tray and these cubes used in place of ice. This drink can also be made with other frozen juice concentrates such as grape or apple.

1/2	cup	orange juice concentrate
2 1/4	cups	milk, skim or 1%
1		egg*
5		ice cubes

*Use a pasteurized egg or do not use an egg with this recipe

1. In a blender, put the orange juice, milk, and egg. Blend until smooth on medium speed.

2. Add all 5 ice cubes. Blend briefly on low speed and stop. Repeat 3 times, until the ice is crushed. (Or, crush the ice cubes before adding them to the blender.)

3. Pour the mixture in 3 glasses and share it with 2 friends. This is cold but as bright and golden as sunshine.

Yield: 3 (1-cup) servings

	Cal	%Ft	P	F	C
Per Serving	170	11	10	2	29

To make this delicious drink, you have to start the night before.

BANANA BLIZZARD

1	med.	banana, ripe
1	cup	milk, skim or 1%
1/4	cup	vanilla yogurt, low-fat
1/2	tsp.	vanilla extract

1. The night before, peel the banana and cut it into 6 chunks. Put all the banana chunks in a plastic sandwich bag or wrap them in plastic wrap. Put them in the freezer overnight.

2. The next day, put the banana chunks in the blender. Add the milk, yogurt, and vanilla extract.

3. Blend on a low speed until the drink is smooth.

4. When the drink is thick and smooth, turn off the blender. Pour the drink in a glass and enjoy!

Yield: 1 serving

	Cal	%Ft	P	F	C
Per Serving	211	5	12	1	39

ANT HILLS

*This is a filling snack for you
(and for healthy ant eaters).*

2		egg whites
1 1/4	cups	milk, skim or 1%
1/2	cup	applesauce
1	cup	whole wheat flour
2	cups	100% bran cereal
1/3	cup	brown sugar, packed
2	tsp.	baking powder
1/2	tsp.	baking soda
1/2	tsp.	cinnamon
1/2	tsp.	nutmeg
72		raisins (pretend ants)

1. Turn the oven on to 400°. In a large bowl, use an egg separator to separate the yolks from the egg whites. Mix the egg whites, milk, and applesauce together.

2. Add flour, bran cereal, brown sugar, baking powder, baking soda, and spices. Stir until thoroughly mixed.

3. Fill paper-lined muffin pans 2/3 full.

4. Push 3 raisins (ants) into the center of each muffin (the ant hill). Then evenly space 3 raisins (ants) on the top of each muffin.

5. Bake at 400° until slightly brown, about 20 minutes. Be sure to use hotpads when you take these out of the oven. Turn off the oven. Invite friendly ant eaters to join you for breakfast. Serve and enjoy!

Yield: 12 muffins

	Cal	%Ft	P	F	C
Per Muffin	128	2	4	2	28

MONKEY MUFFINS

What a treat!

1	cup	wheat flour
2 1/2	tsp.	baking powder
3/4	cup	rolled oats, quick
1/4	tsp.	salt
1/4	tsp.	baking soda
3	Tbl.	honey
1/2	cup	milk, skim or 1%
1		egg white
1	Tbl.	oil
2		ripe bananas, mashed

Yield: 12 muffins

1. Turn the oven on to 400°. In a large bowl, combine flour, baking powder, rolled oats, salt, and baking soda. Set aside.

2. Use an egg separator to separate the yolk from the egg white. Add the egg white to the flour mixture. Do not mix.

3. Add honey, milk, oil, and bananas to the flour mixture. Stir with a fork until dry ingredients are moistened.

4. Fill paper-lined muffin pans 2/3 full.

5. Bake at 400° until slightly brown, about 18 to 20 minutes. Be sure to use hotpads when you take these out of the oven. Turn off the oven. Cool and serve.

	Cal	%Ft	P	F	C
Per Muffin	**101**	**16**	**3**	**2**	**18**

HOUSE MOUSE
PANCAKES

For fun, use raisins or sliced bananas to make a mouse face on these pancakes.

1 1/3	cups	milk, skim or 1%
2		egg whites
1	tsp.	baking powder
1	Tbl.	oil
1	cup	wheat flour

1. Use an egg separator to separate the yolks from the egg whites. Set egg whites aside.

2. Into a quart jar that has a screw-on lid, pour milk and egg whites. Screw the lid on the jar and shake until milk and egg are thoroughly mixed.

3. Open jar. Set lid aside. Add baking powder and oil. Put the lid back on the jar and shake it again.

4. Open jar. Spoon whole wheat flour in the jar. Put the lid back on the jar and shake it until the flour is thoroughly mixed with the milk. Set the jar aside.

5. Cooking the pancakes works best on a nonstick griddle at 400°. However, you can use a large frying pan. Spray a frying pan with vegetable cooking spray. Turn the stove on to medium high.

6. When the griddle or frying pan is hot, pour the pancake batter on to the hot surface. Each pancake should resemble a mouse head—one large circle for the head and two smaller circles for the ears.

7. When bubbles form on the pancake, turn it over with a large pancake turner. Cook for about 1 minute. Put the cooked pancakes onto a plate until you have cooked as many as you like.

8. Turn off the stove. Serve with Select-A-Topping (pp. 58-60) and a glass of milk.

IDEA: If you do not want to make a mouse, create another animal. Why not try a butterfly or an abominable snowman?

Yield: 8 (1/2-cup) pancakes

	Cal	%Ft	P	F	C
Per Serving	82	22	4	2	13

FRENCH TOAST

*This tongue-twister treat is tough
to say but sweet to eat!*

2		egg whites
2	Tbl.	milk, skim or 1%
1/4	tsp.	vanilla extract
1/8	tsp.	cinnamon
1	slice	whole wheat bread

1. Use an egg separator to separate the yolks from the egg whites. Set egg whites aside.

2. In an 8-inch square baking pan, combine egg whites, milk, vanilla extract, and cinnamon. Beat lightly with a whisk. Set pan aside.

3. Cooking the French toast works best on a nonstick griddle at 400°. However, you can use a large frying pan. Spray a frying pan with vegetable cooking spray. Turn the stove on to medium.

4. Dip the bread slice (both sides) into the egg mixture and place it on the griddle or in the frying pan. Cook it until it is golden brown on one side. Flip it over with a pancake turner and cook until it is golden brown on the other side.

5. Turn off the stove. Put the French toast on a plate and top with Select-A-Topping (pp. 58-60). Serve with a glass of milk. Delicious, but don't try to say "simply scrumptious super sumptuous single simple cinnamon French toast" while you are eating!

Yield: 1 serving

	Cal	%Ft	P	F	C
Per Serving	96	T	10	T	13

SELECT-A-TOPPING

PAINT YOUR PANCAKE

*Go ahead and play in your food
with these great toppings!*

On a Saturday (or when you have about an hour), make this recipe 4 times. Make it once with grape juice, once with apple juice, once with orange juice, and once with pineapple juice. Store each recipe separately in a covered jar in the refrigerator. Then when you make pancakes or French toast and need a topping, all 4 of these will be ready for you to "paint with."

4	cups	fruit juice
4	Tbl.	cornstarch

1. Do not turn on the stove yet. Into a 2-quart saucepan, pour the fruit juice. Add the cornstarch. Use a whisk to mix the cornstarch with the fruit juice.

2. Turn the stove on to high. Use a long-handled wooden spoon to stir this mixture until it boils rapidly.

3. Turn off the stove. Remove the pan from the stove. The fruit syrup is ready to serve. Use a spoon, not a paintbrush, to create your designs on your pancakes or French toast.

IDEA: Have a "Paint Your Pancake" party. See who can create the best design using all 4 toppings, Jam Session (p. 60), raisins, and sliced bananas.

Yield: 4 cups

	Cal	%Ft	P	F	C
Per Cup	82	T	0	T	20

SELECT-A-TOPPING

SIMPLE SASSY SAUCE

*No cooking! Make it ahead
of time and there is no waiting—
just good eating!*

4	cups	applesauce, unsweetened
1/2	cup	frozen orange juice concentrate, thawed
2	tsp.	cinnamon

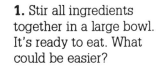

1. Stir all ingredients together in a large bowl. It's ready to eat. What could be easier?

2. Pour 1/2 cup of Simple Sassy Sauce over pancakes or French toast.

3. Store the rest of the sauce in the refrigerator in a covered container. Enjoy—and don't be sassy!

4. IDEA: For other pancake toppings, try Tutti-Frutti Treat (p. 67) or Jam Session (p. 60).

Yield: 8 (1/2-cup) servings

	Cal	%Ft	P	F	C
Per Serving	43	T	0	T	10

TOAST WITH THE MOST

Whole wheat toast is one of the simplest breakfasts you can make. It is good with a glass of milk or a glass of fruit juice. You can spread applesauce on it and add a sprinkle of cinnamon. Or you can use a little Paint Your Pancake (p. 58) or Simple Sassy Sauce (p. 59) on it. If you want jam on your toast, use fresh fruit jams that have low sugar. You can buy them at the grocery store or you can make your own by using the recipe below.

JAM SESSION

This is also good on pancakes or French toast.

1	16-oz. can	peach slices in light syrup
1/2	cup	water
3	Tbl.	cornstarch

1. Do not turn on the stove yet. Pour the can of peaches, including the juice, in to a 2-quart saucepan. Use a dinner knife to cut the peaches into smaller pieces, about 1 inch each. Set aside.

2. Pour 1/2 cup water in a liquid measuring cup. Add the cornstarch and use a whisk to stir the cornstarch in the water.

3. Pour the water and cornstarch mixture over the peaches. Stir together with a long-handled wooden spoon.

4. Turn the stove on to high. Stir constantly until the peaches begin to boil rapidly. Mixture will thicken as soon as it boils. Watch it so it doesn't burn.

5. Turn off the stove. The jam is now ready. Let it cool and store it in the refrigerator in a covered jar.

6. IDEA: Replace the canned peaches with a 20-oz. can of crushed pineapple packed in its own juice. Delicious!

Yield 40 (1-tablespoon) servings

	Cal		%Ft	P	F	C
Per Serving	6		2	0	T	1

"IT'S A SCHOOL DAY"

School days are filled with classrooms, recesses, teachers, friends, papers, pencils, and books. School days are days when you make many choices about what you do.

After-school time is filled with homework or playing with your friends. Some days music lessons or sports may take up your time after school.

School days are also days when you make many choices about what you eat. You may pack your own lunch or you may eat hot lunch at school. Either way, you make your own choices about what you eat. After school, you and your friends probably choose your own snacks.

School days are good days to practice making choices. This chapter has ideas to help you make good choices. It suggests foods you can take with you in the morning so you don't have to skip breakfast (see p. 63). It also has ideas for eating lunch at school or for packing your own lunch to take to school (see pp. 64-65).

When you make good choices, you will feel better about yourself. Eating nutritious foods will help you do many things better, such as play ball, jump rope, or learn in school. And you'll be developing habits that will help you all your life. So take time to think about the choices you make on school days and make the best choices you can.

SCHOOL BUS BREAKFASTS

On some days, it's just easier to eat breakfast on the way to school. You may walk, ride a bike, or ride on a school bus or in a car. The important thing is to eat breakfast. Following are some ideas.

1 Fresh fruit, such as a banana or an apple (p. 12)

2 Dry cereal in a plastic container (p. 50)

3 Ant Hills (p. 54) or Monkey Muffins (p. 55)

4 Toast and jam (see Jam Session, p. 60)

5 Coney Island Cone (p. 74)

6 Spare Parts (p. 78)

7 Pick Pockets (p. 80)

8 Snic Snac Bars (p. 103)

9 A slice of whole grain bread (see "No Need to Knead" Bread, p. 120)

Whether you take your lunch to school in a paper sack or a lunch box, you can take just about anything you want to. Just plan ahead so that your lunches will be tasty and nutritious. Following are some suggestions:

1 If you have a thermos, you can take soup, chili, stew, warm drinks, or leftovers from last night's dinner. Or you can take cold milk or fruit juice.

2 Use plastic containers with tight-fitting lids to take applesauce, chopped melon, crushed pineapple, canned pears, or canned peaches.

3 Fresh fruit is an excellent choice for school lunch. It is easy to pack and easy to eat. And it stays fresh. Try an apple, banana, orange, plum, peach, tangerine, or grapes. A whole tomato is delicious, also.

4 Fresh vegetables are also an excellent choice for school lunch. Carrots, celery, cucumbers, broccoli, or cauliflower can be packed in a plastic container with a tight-fitting lid. You could also pack vegetable dip in another plastic container.

5 Whole wheat bread or muffins travel to school easily in a plastic sandwich bag. Buy a carton of milk at school to drink with the bread or muffins.

7 Sandwiches are a school lunch favorite. Use whole grain bread. Fill your sandwich with low-fat items such as chicken, turkey, tuna, tomatoes, or sprouts. Be daring and try a banana sandwich or a cucumber sandwich. Peanut butter is high in fat, so use just a little bit in your sandwich. Use fresh fruit jam with little or no sugar.

8 Take Geometry Chips (p. 71) in a plastic sandwich bag, and salsa or low-fat refried beans in a plastic container.

6 Use a plastic container to take cereal (see p. 50). Buy milk at school to pour over the top of the cereal. The plastic container becomes a bowl. Bring a plastic spoon with you.

FUNNY-FACE SANDWICH

*Make ugly faces, funny
faces, or animal faces! Then
eat them when you are done.*

1 slice whole wheat bread, toasted

2 Tbl. applesauce, unsweetened

Plus Face-Maker Foods:

  banana slices

  raisins or dates

  nuts

  shredded coconut

Yield: 1 serving

1. Toast the bread.

2. Spread 2 tablespoons
applesauce on the toast.

3. Use bananas, raisins, dates,
nuts, or coconut to make a face
on your toast before you eat it.

4. ZOO ANIMALS: Use
cookie cutters on the plain
toast and cut out animal
shapes. Then spread
applesauce on the animals
and decorate them with
pieces of banana, raisins,
dates, nuts, or shredded
coconut. You can make your
own zoo. Have fun!

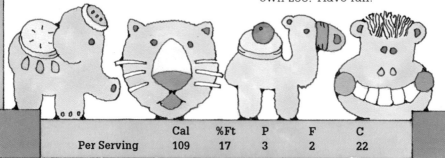

	Cal	%Ft	P	F	C
Per Serving	109	17	3	2	22

TUTTI-FRUTTI TREAT

This is also delicious as a pancake topping.

1/2	med.	red apple, unpeeled and chopped
1	cup	applesauce, unsweetened
1/4	cup	crushed pineapple, drained
1/8	cup	raisins
1/4	tsp.	cinnamon
6	Tbl.	vanilla yogurt, low-fat

1. Into a medium-sized bowl, put the chopped apple.

2. Add the applesauce, pineapple, raisins, and cinnamon to the chopped apples.

Stir together. You can eat it now or chill it in the refrigerator for 2 hours.

3. Serve this with 1 tablespoon yogurt on top.

Yield: 6 (1/4-cup) servings

	Cal	%Ft	P	F	C
Per Serving	45	5	1	T	9

1 POTATO, 2 POTATO, 3 POTATO, 4

Keep baked potatoes in the refrigerator so you'll be ready to make this treat at a moment's notice.

2	med.	potatoes, baked
2	Tbl.	apple juice or BBQ sauce
1	tsp.	seasoning (p. 36)

1. The night before, wash 4 potatoes. Put them on a baking sheet, whole and with the skins left on. Bake them in the oven at 350° for 1 hour. Use hotpads to take them out of the oven. Let them cool. Put them in the refrigerator overnight.

2. The next day after school, turn the oven on to 400°. Then take the potatoes out of the refrigerator and slice them lengthwise into 4 wedges.

3. Place the potato pieces into a large bowl. Add apple juice or barbecue sauce. Stir with a large spoon until each potato piece is evenly covered with the juice.

4. Use a slotted spoon to scoop the potato wedges out of the liquid. Put them into another large bowl. Sprinkle seasonings over the wedges. Stir them until each piece is completely covered. Set bowl aside.

5. Spray a baking sheet with vegetable cooking spray. Spread potato pieces on the baking sheet. Don't let the pieces of potato touch each other.

6. Put the baking sheet in the oven. Bake for 7 minutes.

7. Use hotpads to take the baking sheet out of the oven. Turn the pieces of potato over with a pancake turner. Continue baking for 7 minutes longer. Turn off the oven. Take the baking sheet out of the oven again and enjoy your potato treat. Yummy!

Yield: 2 servings

	Cal	%Ft	P	F	C
Per Serving	152	1	4	T	35

GINGER BITS

Tiny but tasty gingerbread cookies.

1/4	cup	light molasses
1/4	cup	corn oil
1/4	cup	honey
1/3	cup	hot water
1/2	tsp.	salt
1/2	tsp.	baking soda
1	tsp.	ground ginger
1/8	tsp.	ground cloves
1/8	tsp.	nutmeg
1/8	tsp.	allspice
1 1/2	cups	whole wheat flour

1. Turn the oven on to 375°. In a large bowl, stir together molasses, oil, honey, and water until they are thoroughly mixed.

2. Add salt, baking soda, ginger, cloves, nutmeg, and allspice. Mix well.

3. Add flour and stir until thoroughly mixed. The cookie dough should be stiff. If it is not stiff, add more flour (1/4 cup at a time) until it is stiff. Set bowl aside.

4. Spray a baking sheet with vegetable cooking spray. Use a 1 teaspoon measuring spoon to scoop out the cookie dough, and then form it into a small ball with your hands and place it onto the baking sheet. After you have the baking sheet dotted with unbaked cookies, flatten each ball with the bottom of a glass.

5. Bake at 375° for 10 minutes. Use hotpads to remove the baking sheet from the oven. Use a pancake turner to move the cookies from the baking sheet to a rack. Let the cookies cool. Enjoy!

6. Repeat steps 4 and 5 until the cookie dough is baked. (Or you can store the cookie dough in the refrigerator and bake it tomorrow.) Store leftover cookies in a covered container.

Yield: 25 cookies

	Cal	%Ft	P	F	C
Per Cookie	**62**	**33**	**1**	**2**	**10**

UP AND DOWN THE SCALES

Fruit or vegetables lined up in an even, orderly pattern on a stick are pretty to look at, fun to make, and delicious to eat.

Toothpicks or bamboo skewers

For Fruit Kabobs use any of the following:

1-inch chunks of pineapple, apples, cheese, melon, whole grapes, cherries, strawberries, or orange sections.

For Vegetable Kabobs use any of the following:

1-inch chunks of cucumber, onion, bell pepper, cooked chicken, squash, whole cherry tomatoes, or mushrooms.

1. Wash fruits and vegetables. Set whole fruits and vegetables aside. Cut other fruits and vegetables into 1-inch chunks.

2. Alternate pieces of fruit on a toothpick or a bamboo skewer to make a fruit kabob. You can chill these in the refrigerator before eating, if you like.

3. Alternate pieces of vegetables on a toothpick or a bamboo

skewer to make a vegetable kabob. You can heat these in the oven at 350° for a few minutes, if you like. Watch them, and take them out when the vegetables go limp.

4. Remember, practice makes perfect in anything you do, whether it's lining up fruits and vegetables on a stick, practicing scales on the piano, or shooting baskets.

Yield: As many as you want to make. No fat.

GEOMETRY CHIPS

12   corn   tortillas

Happy homework! Who would have guessed geometry could "taste" so good?

1. Turn the oven on to 300°.

2. Spray a baking sheet with vegetable cooking spray or use a nonstick baking sheet.

3. Use kitchen scissors or a knife to cut each corn tortilla into 6 geometric shapes—triangles, squares, or circles. Try to cut the pieces to about the same size so that they will cook evenly. Place the shapes on the baking sheet.

4. Put the baking sheet in the oven. Bake the chips for 8 to 10 minutes.

5. WATCH THESE CLOSELY! The chips will burn easily. Use hotpads to take the baking sheet out of the oven. Pour the chips into a bowl.

6. Repeat steps 2 through 5 until all the chips are toasted.

7. These chips taste great dipped in salsa or low-fat refried beans. Store the leftover chips in a covered container.

8. IDEA: Try a sprinkle of your favorite seasoning (see p. 36) to give these chips a spicy taste.

Yield: 6 (12-chip) servings

	Cal	%Ft	P	F	C
Per Serving	110	16	2	2	20

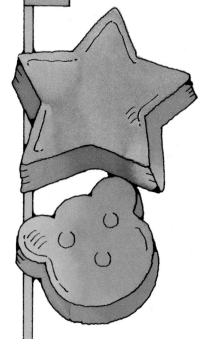

WIGGLE, WAGGLE, JIGGLE, JAGGLE

*Fruit juice gelatin is fun
to make and fun to eat!*

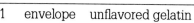

| 1 | envelope | unflavored gelatin |
| 2 | cups | fruit juice (apple, orange, or grape) |

1. Turn on the stove. In a 2-quart saucepan, heat fruit juice until it is just starting to boil. Turn off the stove and set the saucepan aside.

2. Into a medium bowl, pour the unflavored gelatin.

3. Add the hot fruit juice and stir until the gelatin is completely dissolved.

4. Now the fun begins. You can do so many things with this fruit juice gelatin!

Yield: 4 (1/2-cup) servings

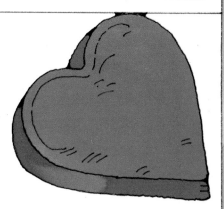

Pour gelatin into a mold. Set mold in the refrigerator and chill until firm. Enjoy!

	Cal	%Ft	P	F	C
Per Serving	82	T	2	T	19

BOINK!

GIGGLES

Pour fruit juice gelatin in a 9" x 13" pan. Chill until firm. Cut gelatin into triangles and eat them with your fingers. Or toss gelatin triangles with fresh fruit such as straw-berries, pieces of banana, grapes, or chopped apples.

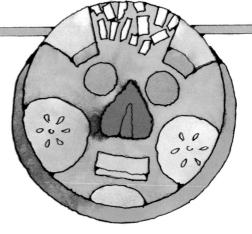

Allow fruit juice gelatin to thicken in the refrigerator. Before it sets, add fruit pieces or shredded vegetables. Make faces or designs.

PATCHWORK

Allow fruit juice gel-atin to thicken in the refrigerator. Before it sets, whip 1/4 cup plain yogurt into it. Set.

Fill a glass half full with fruit juice gelatin. Chill until firm. Add a layer of cottage cheese or yogurt. Top with a layer of chopped fresh fruit.

YIKES!

STRIPES!

MELLOW GELLOW

Freeze fruit juice gelatin in paper cups with a wooden popsicle stick handle.

REBOUNDS

Yield: 4 (1/2-cup) servings

CONEY ISLAND CONE

If your friends like cottage cheese salad, invite them to your house to make Coney Island Cones with you. Then you can all take one with you when you go outside to play.

1	flat-bottomed ice cream cone
1/4 cup	cottage cheese, low-fat

Choose from the following:

1	Tbl.	carrots, grated
1	Tbl.	crushed pineapple, drained
chopped		apples or pears
chopped		celery
1	whole	cherry tomato
6	whole	raisins

Yield: 1 cone

1. Drain the crushed pineapple. Set it aside.

2. Grate part of a washed carrot. Set it aside.

3. Chop celery, apples, pears, or any other fruit or vegetable you would like to add to this salad. Set it aside.

4. Drain the cottage cheese and put 1 scoop (about 1/4 cup) in a small bowl. Add the pineapple and carrots. Stir together.

5. Add any other fruits or vegetables. Stir together.

6. Scoop the cottage cheese mixture into the ice cream cone.

7. Decorate it with a cherry tomato, raisins, or leftover chopped fruits and vegetables. Now it is ready to eat.

8. IDEA: Use the cottage cheese mixture, without the cone, as a stuffing for Tomato Torture Chamber (pp. 86-87), as a vegetable or fruit dip, or as a filling for pocket sandwiches (see Pick Pockets, p. 80).

	Cal	%Ft	P	F	C
Per Serving	16	7	2	T	2

"HOORAY! IT'S THE WEEKEND!"

"HOORAY! IT'S THE WEEKEND!"

Weekends can be fun. Maybe you will invite friends to your house to go bike riding together or to sleep overnight. Perhaps movies, shopping, or a picnic will fill up your time. If you play sports, a game or a practice might fill your Saturday morning.

Weekends can be busy, too. Saturday mornings are often filled with work, like cleaning your bedroom or washing windows. Maybe you have a garden or animals that need tending.

Weekends are also a time to be with family. On Sundays, some families have brunch or dinner together after church. Other families visit relatives or friends. Maybe you will simply stay home and read a book.

However you spend your weekends, cooking can be an important part of them. So wash your hands, put on your apron, and find a recipe that sounds good to you. Weekends are a good time to practice cooking and a good time to share the results. Have fun!

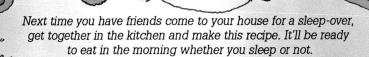

Next time you have friends come to your house for a sleep-over, get together in the kitchen and make this recipe. It'll be ready to eat in the morning whether you sleep or not.

SLEEP-OVER
FRENCH TOAST

6		3/4-inch slices of French bread
1		egg, beaten
4		egg whites, beaten
2	cups	milk, skim or 1%
3/4	tsp.	cinnamon OR
1	tsp.	Gifford's Dessert Spice®

1. Spray a 9" x 13" baking pan with vegetable cooking spray. Arrange bread slices in the baking pan. Set the pan aside.

2. Use an egg separator to separate yolks from egg whites. In a small bowl, use a whisk to stir the whole egg, egg whites, milk, and cinnamon together.

3. Pour the egg mixture over the slices of bread in the baking pan.

4. Cover the baking pan with plastic wrap. Put it in the refrigerator overnight (while you and your friends stay up laughing and talking).

5. In the morning, remove the plastic wrap from the baking pan. Put the pan in the oven and bake at 350° for 30 minutes. Remember to use hotpads when you take the pan out of the oven.

6. Serve the French toast with Select-A-Topping (pp. 58-59). Eat, enjoy, and then GO TO SLEEP!

Yield: 6 (1-slice) servings

	Cal	%Ft	P	F	C
Per Serving	**116**	**14**	**8**	**2**	**17**

SPORTS! SPO

SPARE PARTS

If you use your imagination, the pieces of this mix look like car parts!

1	cup	Wheat Chex
2	cups	Rice Chex
1	cup	Corn Chex
1	cup	Cheerios
2	cups	pretzel sticks
1/3	cup	apple juice
4	tsp.	Worcestershire sauce
1/2	tsp.	garlic powder
1	tsp.	onion powder

1. Turn the oven on to 275°. In a large bowl, combine cereals. Add pretzel sticks. Stir together. Set aside.

2. In a small bowl, mix together apple juice, Worcestershire sauce, garlic powder, and onion powder.

3. Pour the apple juice mixture over the cereals. Stir together until each piece is covered. Set aside.

4. Spray a 9" x 13" baking pan with vegetable cooking spray.

Pour the cereal mixture into the pan and put it in the oven.

5. Set the timer for 10 minutes. Stir the mixture. When the timer rings, put a pretzel stick on the counter.

6. Reset the timer for 10 minutes. Repeat step 5 until you have 6 pretzels on the counter (1 hour).

7. Let the pan cool on a rack for 30 minutes. Pour mix into a bowl and enjoy.

8. IDEA: In a microwaveable dish, cook at full power for 6 minutes. Stir every 2 minutes.

9. IDEA: Want a great gift idea? Fill a glass jar with Spare Parts. Tie a ribbon around the jar. Now you have a terrific gift for a friend, neighbor, or teacher.

Yield: 7 (1-cup) servings

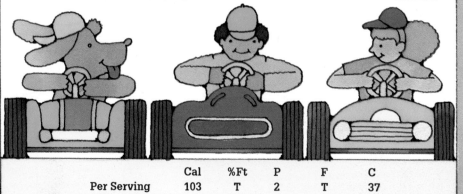

	Cal	%Ft	P	F	C
Per Serving	103	T	2	T	37

ICE HOCKEY

This healthful treat makes a versatile snack or an unusual breakfast.

1		banana, very ripe and peeled
1/2	cup	orange juice
1/4	cup	lemon juice
2	cups	pineapple juice
2 1/2	cups	crushed ice and water

1. In a blender, blend banana, orange juice, and lemon juice on medium speed until smooth. Pour the banana mixture into a large bowl. Add the pineapple juice and stir until smooth. Set aside.

2. In another large bowl, combine crushed ice with a little water until you have a total of 2 1/2 cups of slush.

3. Add the banana mixture to the slush. Stir thoroughly. This icy drink is ready to keep you cool. Serve. Freeze any leftovers (see step 4).

4. OR freeze the mixture in a wide, unbreakable bowl or pan. Scrape frozen fruit mixture out with an ice cream scoop or spoon and put it into a glass. Pour carbonated water over the top and serve.

5. OR make popsicles. Fill paper cups with the slush. Put a spoon or a popsicle stick into each cup. Freeze. To eat, tear the paper cup from the frozen fruit juice and hold on to the handle so you can lick the frozen popsicle.

Yield: 5 (1-cup) servings

	Cal	%Ft	P	F	C
Per Serving	70	2	1	T	18

PICK POCKETS

Pick your favorite sandwich filling to fill these pocket sandwiches.

1	piece	pita bread

Choose your fillings:

  sprouts or lettuce

  chunks of cooked chicken or turkey

  chopped celery, apples, tomatoes, cucumbers, mushrooms

  garbanzo beans or kidney beans, cooked and chilled

  grated cheese

  cottage cheese and crushed pineapple

  canned low-fat salsa and refried beans

Yield: 2 pocket sandwiches

1. Pick the filling you want in your pocket sandwich. Prepare the filling and set it aside. Remember to keep the filling moist so that your pocket sandwich won't taste dry. Use low-fat ranch dressing, tomatoes, cottage cheese, or Dilly Dip (p. 85) to help keep it moist.

2. Cut the pita bread in half. Each half circle will open into a pocket.

3. Fill the pocket with your favorite filling. Eat it and enjoy! Next time you can pick another "pocket" filling.

4. IDEA: Fill your pocket sandwich with a recipe of Coney Island Cone (p. 74), Scrambled Surprise (p. 90), Ham and Green Eggs (p. 98), Happy Holiday Salad (p. 107), Sombrero Salad minus the tortillas (p. 117), Hot-Shot Chili (p. 119), or Apple-Tuna Toss (p. 122).

	Cal	%Ft	P	F	C
Per Serving	135	22	11	3	18

PITA PIZZA

You'll enjoy this noontime treat after spending Saturday morning cleaning your bedroom.

1	piece	pita bread
1/2	cup	low-fat refried beans
2	Tbl.	mozzarella cheese, shredded
		salsa (optional)

Choose your toppings:

chopped celery, onions, tomatoes, green bell peppers, mushrooms; look for leftover vegetables, such as corn, in your refrigerator.

1. Turn on the broiler.

Yield: 1 Pita Pizza

2. Prepare the toppings you want on your Pita Pizza. Set them aside.

3. Put the pita bread on the broiler pan. Spread the refried beans on top of the slice of pita bread. Sprinkle chopped toppings or leftover vegetables on the refried beans. Sprinkle the cheese over the toppings.

4. Put it under the broiler until the cheese melts (about 3 minutes). Use hotpads to remove the broiler pan from the oven. Use a pancake turner to move the Pita Pizza from the broiler pan to your plate. Top with salsa. Cut it into pie-shaped pieces using a pizza cutter. Enjoy! Now, doesn't it feel good to have a clean bedroom?

5. IDEA: Heat this in a microwave oven until the cheese melts (about 1 minute) if you want a softer Pita Pizza.

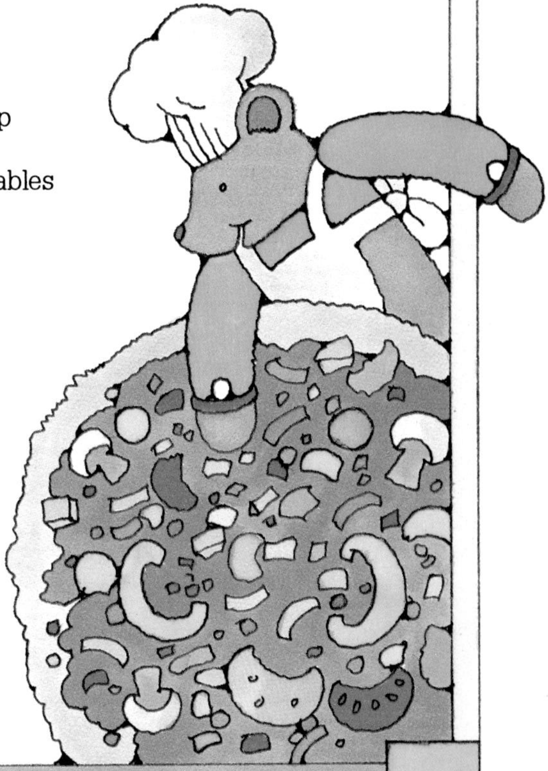

	Cal	%Ft	P	F	C
Per Pizza	301	11	16	4	50

SUNSHINE POPS

Easy for you to make and good for you to eat.

2	cups	orange juice
1/2	cup	vanilla yogurt, low-fat

1. In a blender, blend orange juice and yogurt on high speed.

2. Pour the mixture into 6 small paper cups. Put a plastic spoon or a popsicle stick in each cup.

3. Put the cups into the freezer. Let them freeze overnight.

4. The following day, the popsicles will be ready. Peel the paper cup off the popsicle just before you eat it. These will taste especially good when you are hot and tired after working around the house or playing with your friends.

Yield: 6 popsicles

	Cal	%Ft	P	F	C
Per Serving	47	13	1	1	10

THE HOUSE

WINTER WARM-UP

Drink this after sledding, shoveling snow, ice skating, or building a snowman. It will warm you up.

1	10-oz. can	beef broth
1	10-oz. soup	can water
1	cup	vegetable juice

1. Do not turn the stove on yet. In a 2-quart saucepan, stir all the ingredients together with a long-handled wooden spoon.

2. Turn the stove on to medium. Stir mixture occasionally until warm (about 5 minutes).

3. Turn off the stove. Use a ladle to pour the mixture into a mug. Drink it while it is warm. Are you ready to go back outside?

Yield: 4 (1-cup) servings

	Cal	%Ft	P	F	C
Per Serving	21	13	2	T	3

WHEELS, WHIRLS, AND CURLS

It's fun to eat fancy raw vegetables.

CUCUMBER WHEELS

1	cucumber, cold

Peel completely. Using a fork, pull tines down the cucumber lengthwise. Repeat until ridges completely cover cucumber. Slice crosswise. Serve.

	Cal	%Ft	P	F	C
Per Serving	30	T	T	T	6

RADISH WHIRLS

5	radishes

Wash and cut off the top of the radishes so that some white shows. Make 3 evenly spaced diagonal cuts lengthwise near the edge. Chill in ice water until crisp. Serve.

	Cal	%Ft	P	F	C
Per Serving	20	T	T	T	5

CARROT CURLS

1	carrot

Peel carrot. Slice it paper-thin lengthwise with a vegetable peeler. Roll each curl up and fasten it with a toothpick. Leave in ice water until curled. Remove toothpick before serving.

	Cal	%Ft	P	F	C
Per Serving	60	T	2	T	14

VEGGIE ROBOTS

Take some time to play with your veggie robots before you eat them.

1. Use several kinds of raw vegetables. Wash them carefully.

2. Create robots using whole vegetables and pieces of vegetables attached to each other with toothpicks.

3. Eat the robots when you are finished playing. Remember to take out the toothpicks before you bite into the robot.

DILLY DIP

This also tastes good on a tossed salad.

2/3	cup	cottage cheese, low-fat
1/3	cup	plain yogurt, low-fat
1	tsp.	lemon juice
1	tsp.	dill seed
1	tsp.	minced dried onion

1. In a blender, blend cottage cheese, yogurt, lemon juice, dill seed, and onion.

2. Blend on high speed until smooth. You may need to turn off the blender, open it, and stir the mixture with a long-handled wooden spoon. Be careful. When you are finished, put the lid back on the blender and run it again.

3. When the mixture is smooth, use a rubber scraper to scrape mixture off the sides of the blender into a bowl.

4. Dip vegetables into this mixture for a "dilly" taste. Crunch and munch. Store leftover dip in a covered container in the refrigerator.

Yield: 16 (1-tablespoon) servings

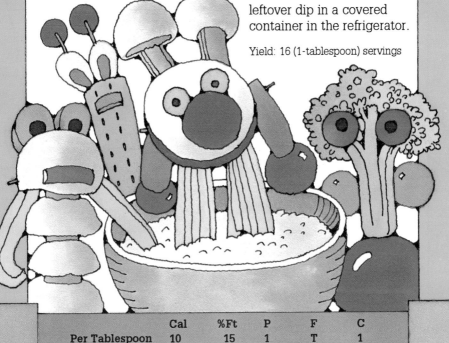

	Cal	%Ft	P	F	C
Per Tablespoon	10	15	1	T	1

TOMATO TORTURE

STUFF 'EM

Don't be too cruel. Just cut them apart and stuff 'em full!

1	medium	tomato, firm

Yield: 1 serving

1. Wash the tomato.

2. Cut it into 6 wedges, but only cut 3/4 of the way through so that it resembles a flower. (Or cut it in half lengthwise and scoop out the pulp.)

3. Stuff the tomato with cottage cheese, Coney Island Cone filling (p. 74), tuna salad, or chicken salad. Enjoy!

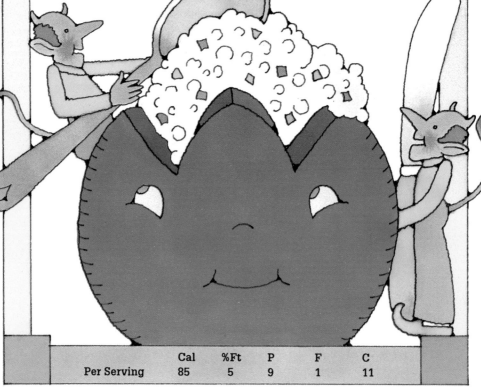

	Cal	%Ft	P	F	C
Per Serving	85	5	9	1	11

CHAMBER
BROIL 'EM

Don't be too cruel. Just cut them in half and broil 'em!

1	med.	tomato, firm
1	Tbl.	topping: Parmesan cheese
	or	bread crumbs
	or	shredded mozzarella cheese

1. Turn on the broiler.

2. Wash the tomato. Cut it in half lengthwise. Place it on a broiler pan.

3. Sprinkle a topping on each half of the tomato. Put the tomatoes under the broiler and broil for 2 minutes. Don't let them burn. Enjoy!

Yield: 1 serving

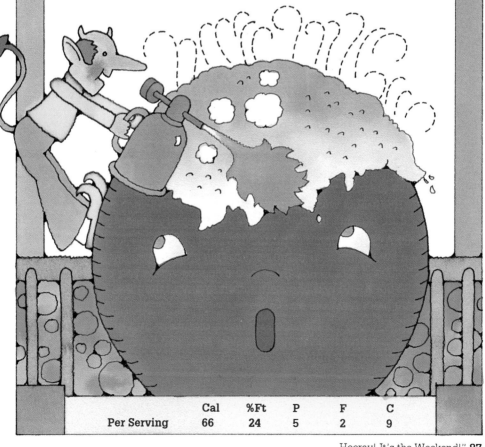

	Cal	%Ft	P	F	C
Per Serving	66	24	5	2	9

TIC- TAC- TOE
FRUIT COMBO

*Just make sure the fruit
is fresh and ripe and cut into
bite-sized pieces.*

1. Just about any combination of fresh fruit tastes great. Make sure the fruit is washed or peeled, or cut it into 1-inch pieces. Put fruit together in any combination to equal 3 cups.

2. IDEA: Play a game of tic-tac-toe with one of your friends. Then lay the finished game next to this chart. If you are the "X," choose fruit in any three of the spaces where you put an "X." Your friend can choose the fruit in any of the three spaces where he or she puts an "O."

3. IDEA: Close your eyes and touch a picture of fruit on this tic-tac-toe board. Do it 2 more times. Now you have a combination of 3 fruits for your "fruit combo."

Yield: 6 (1/2-cup) servings

	Cal	%Ft	P	F	C
Per Serving	66	2	T	1	16

ORANGE DIP

Simple to make. Delicious to eat!

1/2 cup	vanilla yogurt, low-fat
1/2 tsp.	orange peel
1/2 tsp.	orange flavor extract (optional)

1. In a small bowl, mix yogurt and flavorings.

2. Fresh fruit dip is ready to use. Store leftover dip in the refrigerator in a covered container.

Yield: 8 (1-tablespoon) servings

	Cal	%Ft	P	F	C
Per Tablespoon	8	29	1	T	1

S U N D A Y

SCRAMBLED SURPRISE

Top this with salsa for a south-of-the-border flavor.

2		egg whites
1		egg
1	Tbl.	water
1	Tbl.	onions, chopped
1	Tbl.	green pepper, chopped
1/2		tomato, chopped
to taste		seasonings (p. 36)

1. Use an egg separator to separate yolks and egg whites. In a deep bowl, beat egg whites, egg, and water together with a fork or an electric mixer until foamy.

2. Add chopped vegetables. Set aside.

3. Spray a frying pan with vegetable cooking spray. Pour egg mixture into the frying pan and scramble over medium heat until eggs are cooked.

4. Serve with Skillet Skitters (p. 91).

Yield: 1 serving

5. IDEA: Turn this into an egg sandwich by putting it between two slices of bread or in a pocket sandwich (see Pick Pockets, p. 80).

	Cal	%Ft	P	F	C
Per Serving	127	43	13	6	6

SKILLET SKITTERS

When you cook food in a nonstick pan and use chicken bouillon instead of oil, you don't add any fat.

2	med.	potatoes, baked
1/2	small	onion, chopped (optional)
1/4	cup	chicken bouillon
to taste		seasonings (p. 36)

1. Bake the potatoes the night before for 1 hour at 350°. Put them in the refrigerator overnight. (You may want to bake 6 or 8 potatoes. Then next time you want to make hash browns, you will already have cooked potatoes.)

2. Slice the baked potatoes into pieces that look like half circles. (Cut the potato lengthwise. Then cut it crosswise every 1/4 inch.) Leave the skins on the potatoes. Combine the potatoes and the chopped onions in a bowl. Set it aside.

3. Don't turn the stove on yet. Spray a nonstick frying pan (skillet) with vegetable cooking spray. Pour in chicken bouillon.

4. Turn the stove on to medium. Add the potato mixture. Add seasonings. Cook until the potatoes are golden brown, turning them often with a pancake turner. Serve for breakfast, lunch, or dinner.

Yield: 2 (1-cup) servings

	Cal	%Ft	P	F	C
Per Serving	156	1	5	T	35

PICNIC CHICKEN STICKS

*Nothing tastes better at a picnic
than chicken drumsticks, and you
can make them!*

1/2	cup	corn flakes, crushed
1/4	cup	whole wheat flour
1	Tbl.	parsley, minced (optional)
1/2	tsp.	paprika
2		egg whites, lightly beaten
1/4	cup	milk, skim or 1%
6		chicken drumsticks

1. Turn the oven on to 375°. In a medium-sized bowl, stir together crushed corn flakes, flour, parsley, and paprika until thoroughly mixed. Set the bowl aside.

2. Use an egg separator to separate yolks and egg whites. In another medium-sized bowl, use a whisk to mix the egg whites with the milk. Set the bowl aside.

3. Spray an 8" x 8" baking pan with vegetable cooking spray. Set the pan aside.

4. Pull the skin off the drumsticks. Dip each drumstick in the bowl of milk and eggs. Then dip it in the bowl of crushed corn flakes. Roll the drumstick around in the mixture so it is evenly coated.

5. Place each drumstick in the baking pan. When all 6 drumsticks are coated, place the baking pan in the oven. Bake the chicken uncovered at 375° for 70 minutes. Do not turn.

6. Turn off the stove. Use hot-pads when you take the pan out of the oven. Take the drumsticks out of the pan and let them cool. Then, you can put them in the refrigerator until you are ready to go on your picnic.

7. When you are ready to go on your picnic, put the drumsticks in a plastic container with a lid or wrap them in aluminum foil. Take them on your picnic, eat them with your hands, and lick your fingers all you want.

8. IDEA: Make a batch of these drumsticks for school lunch. Store them in the refrigerator in a covered container. Then eat them for an after-school snack.

Yield: 6 drumsticks

	Cal	%Ft	P	F	C
Per Serving	119	32	14	4	6

"HAPPY HOLIDAYS"

Almost everyone loves a holiday.
It's a time when we can be
together with our friends or family and enjoy
holiday traditions. Most holiday traditions include food.
This chapter is filled with recipes that can become part of your
holiday tradition. They are simple enough for you to make and
tasty enough that your friends and family will enjoy them
with you.

Grape Juice Razzle Dazzle can be enjoyed after school, at a
birthday party, or with lunch.

I Love Pizza is good anytime for lunch, dinner, or a snack.

Hen on a Nest is an unusual chicken casserole. It is easy to
make and has a tangy taste that will make it a family favorite.

Surprise your mother with breakfast in bed on Mother's Day.
She'll get a good laugh when you serve her Ham and Green
Eggs, but it tastes great.

Let your dad know he's your hero with a "My Hero"
Sandwich. It's big enough for the whole family.

The yummy salads in Four Seasons of Salads are delicious
any time of the year for a snack or a dessert.

If you are lucky enough to have a backyard barbecue or go
camping over the Fourth of July, then you'll want to make Foil
Fireworks for everyone. These are easy to make and delicious.

Snic Snac Bars made from granola can be eaten on a summer
hike. They are also good for breakfast.

Halloween costumes, trick or treats, and a pumpkin full of
Jack-O'-Lantern Soup will make October 31 a night to
remember.

For Thanksgiving, it's a good idea to double or triple the
recipe for Happy Holiday Salad so there will be plenty to go
around. Keep any leftovers in a covered container in the
refrigerator. It makes a great snack.

Wacky Wassail gets its name because you drink it through a
cinnamon stick. Drink it hot or cold, but have fun either way.

Happy holidays! But don't wait until the holidays to enjoy
these recipes.

HAPPY NEW YEAR

GRAPE JUICE RAZZLE DAZZLE

JANUARY						
						1
2	3	4	5	6	7	8
9	10	11	12	13	14	15
16	17	18	19	20	21	22
23/30	24/31	25	26	27	28	29

You can "razzle dazzle" any fruit juice by using 1 cup of any fruit juice and carbonated water.

1	cup	grape juice, unsweetened
1	cup	carbonated water (club soda, seltzer, mineral water)
		crushed ice

1. Pour grape juice in to a pitcher.

2. Slowly add carbonated water. Stir gently.

3. Fill a glass with crushed ice and pour Grape Juice Razzle Dazzle over it. Happy New Year!

Yield: 2 (1-cup) servings

	Cal	%Ft	P	F	C
Per Serving	84	T	0	T	21

I LOVE PIZZA

It's Valentine's Day, the day of love, and what do we love more than pizza?

FEBRUARY

		1	2	3	4	5
6	7	8	9	10	11	12
13	14	15	16	17	18	19
20	21	22	23	24	25	26
27	28					

1	piece	pita bread
1/4	cup	pizza sauce
1/4	cup	low-fat cottage cheese
1	Tbl.	mozzarella cheese

1. Turn the oven on to 400°. Place pita bread on a baking pan. Set aside.

2. In a small bowl, combine 1/4 cup pizza sauce and 1/4 cup cottage cheese. Pour mixture over the pita bread. Use a spoon to spread the sauce evenly.

3. On top, sprinkle chopped onions, green pepper, pine-apple chunks, 2 tablespoons of chopped low-fat ham or cooked hamburger, or mushrooms.

4. Sprinkle mozzarella cheese over the top of everything. Bake at 400° for 15 minutes. Use hot-pads to remove the baking sheet from the oven.

5. Turn the oven off. Use a pan-cake turner to move the pita pizza to a plate. Cut it with a pizza cutter or eat it whole.

6. IDEA: If you have leftover mashed potatoes in the refrigerator, pat them into an 8-inch pie pan. Add pizza sauce, toppings, and cheese. Bake at 400° for 15 minutes. You can't eat it with your hands, but you'll love how it tastes.

7. IDEA: Use a toasted English muffin. Top each half with 1 tablespoon pizza sauce, 1 tablespoon low-fat cottage cheese, and 2 teaspoons mozzarella cheese. Broil until cheese melts, about 5 minutes.

Yield: 1 Pizza

	Cal	%Ft	P	F	C
Per Pizza	263	24	18	7	37

HEN ON A NEST

APRIL						
					1	2
3	4	5	6	7	8	9
10	11	12	13	14	15	16
17	18	19	20	21	22	23
24	25	26	27	28	29	30

This recipe for baked chicken in a tangy sauce nestled on a nest of rice is easy to make for an Easter Sunday dinner.

1		6-oz. can orange juice concentrate, thawed
3		chicken breasts, skinned
1	pkg.	onion soup mix
3	cups	Rodeo Rice (p. 115)

Yield: 6 servings

1. Turn the oven on to 400°. In a small bowl, combine orange juice concentrate and dry onion soup mix. Pour half of mixture into an 8" x 8" nonstick casserole.

2. Place chicken breasts, meat side down, into the casserole and top with remaining sauce.

3. Cover casserole with a lid or foil. Bake at 400° for 1 hour. Use hotpads to take this out of the oven.

4. Cut chicken breasts in half before serving. Scoop rice on to a plate, then place the chicken on its "nest." Top with remaining sauce.

5. IDEA: Replace Rodeo Rice with mashed potatoes or with pasta. Try curly pasta, angelhair pasta, or small egg noodles for the "nest" (p. 118.)

With Rice Per Serving	Cal	%Ft	P	F	C
	184	14	15	3	24
With Potatoes Per Serving	Cal	%Ft	P	F	C
	211	14	16	3	29
With Noodles Per Serving	Cal	%Ft	P	F	C
	243	14	17	4	34

MOTHER'S DAY

HAM AND GREEN EGGS

MAY

1	2	3	4	5	6	7
8	9	10	11	12	13	14
15	16	17	18	19	20	21
22	23	24	25	26	27	28
29	30	31				

2	egg whites
1	egg
2	Tbl. low-fat ham, chopped
1/2	tsp. savory OR
2	drops green food coloring

Surprise your mother on Mother's Day with breakfast in bed.

1. Use an egg separator to separate the yolks from the egg whites. Put the egg whites in a small bowl.

2. Add a whole egg to the egg whites. Use a whisk to mix them together. Set bowl aside.

3. Chop a piece of low-fat ham into 1/2-inch chunks. Set them aside.

4. Spray a frying pan with vegetable cooking spray and put on the stove. Turn heat on to medium. Pour the eggs in to the frying pan and scramble the eggs.

5. Turn the heat down to low before the eggs are completely cooked. Add the ham and savory. Continue to scramble until the mixture is ready to eat. The eggs will turn green. (If you do not have savory, use food coloring.)

6. Serve this with a slice of toast. Be sure to kiss your mother and tell her you love her.

Yield: 1 serving

	Cal	%Ft	P	F	C
Per Serving	133	51	16	8	0

FATHER'S DAY

JUNE

			1	2	3	4
5	6	7	8	9	10	11
12	13	14	15	16	17	18
19	20	21	22	23	24	25
26	27	28	29	30		

"MY HERO"
SANDWICH

Perfect for your hero on Father's Day.

1 loaf	French bread, sliced lengthwise
6 slices	packaged chicken, cooked and sliced
	mustard

Choose any of the following:

- lettuce leaves and alfalfa sprouts
- tomatoes, sliced
- onion, thinly sliced
- pickles, sliced
- cucumbers, sliced
- mushrooms, sliced

1. Slice open the loaf of French bread. Spread mustard on one side of the loaf.

2. Cover the bottom half of the loaf of bread with a layer of lettuce, sprouts, tomatoes, onion slices, pickles, cucumbers, mushrooms, and chicken.

3. Put the top of the loaf back onto the sandwich. Cut it into 6 pieces.

Yield: 6 servings

	Cal	%Ft	P	F	C
Per Serving	260	12	14	4	44

FOUR SEASONS

Spring
Sunburst

Like a sunburst of color, this salad reminds us of springtime sunshine after gray winter days.

1	orange, peeled and sectioned
1	red apple, unpeeled and sliced
2	leaves lettuce
2 Tbl.	crushed pineapple, drained

1. Peel and separate oranges into segments. Set aside.

2. Core unpeeled apples and slice into wedges. Set aside.

3. Lay a lettuce leaf on a salad plate. Then alternate orange segments and apple wedges on the lettuce leaf to form a sunburst.

4. Put a spoonful of crushed pineapple in the center of the sunburst.

5. IDEA: Slice apples and oranges crosswise in thin circles and alternate to form another colorful pattern.

Yield: 2 servings

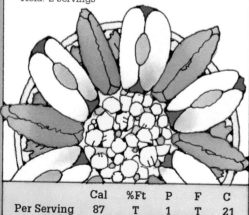

	Cal	%Ft	P	F	C
Per Serving	87	T	1	T	21

Summer
Ring-Around-the-Rosy

This salad reminds us of the fun of playing outside in the summer sunshine.

2	slices	cantaloupe, 1 inch thick
1	cup	strawberries

1. Cut melon crosswise into rings 1 inch thick. Remove seeds.

2. Place rings on individual plates and cut around the slice 1/4 inch from the rind. Do not remove rind but slice the melon into bite-sized pieces, leaving rind intact.

3. Rinse strawberries, but do not remove green stem. Arrange 5 or 6 strawberries in the center of each melon slice. Serve.

Yield: 2 servings

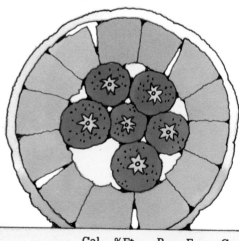

	Cal	%Ft	P	F	C
Per Serving	45	10	1	1	10

OF SALADS

Autumn
Indian Summer

This salad has the bright, warm colors of Indian summer.

1/2	cup	crushed pineapple, drained
2	cups	carrots, shredded
1/4	cup	raisins

1. Drain pineapple. Set it aside.

2. Wash and shred the carrots. Set them aside.

3. In a medium-sized bowl, mix pineapple, carrots, and raisins.

4. Serve on a plate over a lettuce leaf. You can chill this in the refrigerator for 2 hours before serving if you like.

Yield: 2 (1-cup) servings

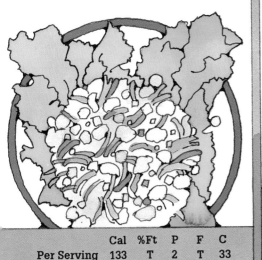

	Cal	%Ft	P	F	C
Per Serving	133	T	2	T	33

Winter
Alpine Ski Slopes

Fresh fruit over a snowy mount of cottage cheese. Fast and fabulous!

1	cup	cottage cheese, low-fat
1		pear, sliced OR
1		peach, sliced

1. Place a lettuce leaf on a plate. Scoop 1/2 cup cottage cheese onto the lettuce leaf.

2. Spoon pear slices or peach slices over the top of the cottage cheese.

3. Eat immediately, or chill in the refrigerator for 2 hours before serving.

Yield: 2 (1/2-cup) servings

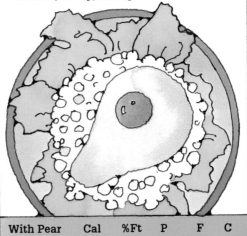

	Cal	%Ft	P	F	C
With Pear Per Serving	140	6	15	1	17
With Peach Per Serving	123	7	15	1	12

FOIL FIREWORKS

JULY						
					1	2
3	4	5	6	7	8	9
10	11	12	13	14	15	16
17	18	19	20	21	22	23
24/31	25	26	27	28	29	30

This is an easy dinner for any Fourth of July picnic—in the mountains, at the beach, or in your own backyard. Enjoy the fireworks!

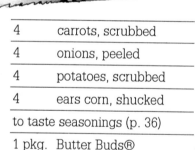

4	carrots, scrubbed
4	onions, peeled
4	potatoes, scrubbed
4	ears corn, shucked
to taste seasonings (p. 36)	
1 pkg.	Butter Buds®

1. Have an adult build a fire or light your barbecue. While the coals are getting hot, cut 4 large aluminum foil squares. Spray the inside with vegetable cooking spray. Set them aside.

2. Cut carrots, onions, and potatoes into 1-inch chunks. Place 1 ear of corn on each square of foil with similar amounts of carrots, onions, and potatoes.

3. Sprinkle 1 tablespoon water and powdered Butter Buds® over the vegetables. Season.

4. Wrap the vegetables snugly in aluminum foil and seal tightly. Place them in the hot coals for 45 to 60 minutes or until vegetables are tender. Turn them occasionally so that they will cook evenly. But be careful; be sure to use hotpads and a flat stick. Serve.

Yield: 4 servings

	Cal	%Ft	P	F	C
Per Serving	291	10	9	3	66

SUMMER HIKE
SNIC SNAC BARS

Eat these for breakfast-on-the-go, put them in your lunch, or enjoy them after school. You could even take them with you on a Saturday hike.

2	cups	low-fat granola, packaged
1		egg
2		egg whites

1. Turn the oven on to 350°. Spray an 8" x 8" pan with vegetable cooking spray. Set the pan aside.

2. In a bowl, beat eggs with a whisk or a fork. Pour in the granola. Stir until the granola is thoroughly coated with eggs.

3. Pour the mixture in the 8-inch square pan. Put the pan in the oven and bake the mixture at 350° for 15 minutes.

4. Use hotpads to remove the pan from the oven. While the mixture is still warm, cut it into 8 bars.

5. Carefully remove the bars from the pan with a pancake turner. They may stick. Set them on a rack to cool.

6. When the bars are cool, eat them or wrap them in aluminum foil or plastic wrap to eat later.

7. IDEA: These are great to take to school for lunch.

Yield: 8 (2" x 4") bars

	Cal	%Ft	P	F	C
Per Bar	95	21	3	2	17

BIRTHDAY BANANA SPLIT

*Your friends will love making their own
banana splits at your birthday party.*

1/2	med.	banana, peeled and sliced
1/4	cup	Frozen Fruit Snow (p. 105)
1/8	cup	strawberries, sliced
1/8	cup	other fruit, sliced
2	tsp.	raisins
2	tsp.	walnuts, chopped
2	tsp.	coconut, shredded

1. Make the recipe for Frozen Fruit Snow. Put it in the freezer until it is hard enough to hold its shape.

2. Peel the banana. Cut it lengthwise and place it in a bowl.

3. Put 1 scoop of Frozen Fruit Snow on the sliced banana.

4. Top with sliced strawberries, fresh fruit, raisins, walnuts, and coconut.

5. Enjoy! Happy Birthday!

6. IDEA: Replace the Frozen Fruit Snow with low-fat cottage cheese, and serve this as a fruit salad. Try Jungle Jumble (p. 49) or Happy Holiday Salad (p. 107) as a topping on the cottage cheese.

Yield: 1 serving (Make one for each guest at your party.)

	Cal	%Ft	P	F	C
Per Serving	167	18	3	3	32

FROZEN FRUIT SNOW

*Do you love ice cream? This
thick, cold treat will thrill you!*

1	cup	milk, skim or 1%
2	cups	peaches, canned or fresh, OR
2	cups	strawberries
2	tsp.	sugar (optional)

1. Freeze peaches or strawberries overnight.

2. About 20 minutes before you are ready to make this, take the fruit out of the freezer and let it sit on the kitchen counter.

3. When the fruit has thawed a little bit, pour the milk into a blender.

4. Add slightly thawed frozen fruit slowly.

5. Blend on high speed until fruit is thoroughly mixed. Use a rubber scraper to scrape the mixture in to a glass or a bowl. It will be easy to enjoy this treat!

6. If you are going to use this on Birthday Banana Splits, place mixture in a bowl and put the bowl into the freezer until the Frozen Fruit Snow is hard enough to hold its shape. Store any leftover Frozen Fruit Snow in the freezer.

7. IDEA: Use frozen milk instead of frozen fruit to make this recipe. Freeze milk in ice cube trays. Add fresh fruit. Blend and serve immediately.

Yield: 8 (1/4-cup) servings

	Cal	%Ft	P	F	C
Per Serving	33	T	1	T	8

JACK-O'-LANTERN SOUP

This soup will warm you up after a night of trick-or-treating.

2	Tbl.	flour
1/4	tsp.	ground ginger
2	cups	milk, skim or 1%
1	12-oz.	can pumpkin, canned
1	cup	water
4	tsp.	chicken bouillon, granules
2	tsp.	pumpkin pie spice
1	tsp.	cinnamon
1	tsp.	nutmeg
1	tsp.	lemon peel

garnish—chives or parsley, chopped

OCTOBER

						1
2	3	4	5	6	7	8
9	10	11	12	13	14	15
16	17	18	19	20	21	22
23/30	24/31	25	26	27	28	29

1. (Optional) Before you start making this soup, have an adult help you hollow out a pumpkin and line it with aluminum foil. Then you can serve this soup from the pumpkin.

2. Pour 1/3 cup milk, flour, and ginger into a small bowl. Use a whisk or a fork to mix the flour and ginger into the milk. Set the bowl aside.

3. Don't turn the stove on yet. Into a 2-quart saucepan, pour the canned pumpkin and the milk/flour/ginger mixture. Stir them together with a long-handled wooden spoon.

4. Stir in the remaining 1 2/3 cups milk. Turn the stove on to medium-high. Stir constantly. Do not allow mixture to boil. Cook mixture for 5 or 10 minutes or until it thickens.

5. Add water, chicken bouillon granules, pumpkin pie spice, cinnamon, nutmeg, and lemon peel. Stir. Heat, but do not boil. Turn off the stove.

6. Use a soup ladle to serve this soup from the pumpkin or the pan into bowls. Before serving the soup, decorate it with chives or parsley to look like a jack-o'-lantern face. Happy Halloween!

Yield: 8 (1-cup) servings

	Cal	%Ft	P	F	C
Per Serving	33	T	2	T	5

NOVEMBER

		1	2	3	4	5
6	7	8	9	10	11	12
13	14	15	16	17	18	19
20	21	22	23	24	25	26
27	28	29	30			

HAPPY HOLIDAY SALAD

Try this as a filling in a pocket sandwich (see Pick Pockets, p. 80).

1/2 cup	crushed pineapple, drained
2	red apples, not peeled, chopped
1	stalk celery, chopped
1 Tbl.	walnuts, chopped

1. In a medium-sized bowl, gently stir the pineapple, apples, celery, and walnuts together.

2. Scoop the mixture in to a bowl or on to a salad plate with a lettuce leaf on it. This is a nice addition to any meal, especially Thanksgiving.

Yield: 3 (1-cup) servings

	Cal	%Ft	P	F	C
Per Serving	74	11	1	1	15

WACKY WASSAIL

Why is this "wacky"?
Because you drink it through
a cinnamon stick straw!

2	cups	apple juice
1	cup	orange juice
1/2	cup	water
1/4	cup	lemon juice
1		cinnamon stick
1/2	tsp.	whole cloves

Yield: 4 (1-cup) servings

1. Don't turn the stove on yet. In a 2-quart saucepan, stir the apple juice, orange juice, water, and lemon juice together.

2. Add the cinnamon stick and cloves. Stir.

3. Turn the stove on to medium-low. When liquid starts to get warm, let it heat for 10 minutes.

4. Turn off the stove. Use a slotted spoon or strainer to scoop out the cinnamon stick and cloves. Then use a ladle to fill drinking mugs.

5. Serve it warm. Remember to give everyone a cinnamon stick to use as a straw. Merry Christmas!

6. IDEA: You can make this in the microwave instead. Put all the ingredients in a glass or plastic bowl. Heat until warm, about 3 minutes.

	Cal	%Ft	P	F	C
Per Serving	88	3	1	T	22

"CAN I COOK DINNER TONIGHT?"

"CAN I COOK DINNER TONIGHT?"

You can help make dinner for your whole family by fixing a salad, soup, bread, dessert, or the main course. First, read "Want to Know a Secret?" (p. 37). That chapter has cooking tips, safety tips, pictures of cooking tools, and definitions of cooking terms. Next, have an adult teach you how to turn the stove and oven on and off, if you do not know how. Remember to use hotpads whenever you take something out of the oven or off of the stove.

When it is time to eat dinner, be sure to set the table properly. Following is a drawing of a simple place setting for dinner.

Place the dinner plate about 1 inch from the edge of the table. The dinner fork goes on the left side of the plate, and the knife and spoon go on the right side. Be sure the sharp edge of the knife is toward the plate. Set the glass above the knife and spoon. The napkin goes on the left side of the fork.

Cleaning up the kitchen after you cook dinner is important. Remember to wash the dishes and pans. Wipe off the stove, countertop, and table. Sweep the floor, if needed. You will feel good about yourself after you are finished.

OTHER DINNER IDEAS

In addition to the recipes in this chapter, there are other recipes in this cookbook that you can cook for dinner. Following is a list of other dinner ideas.

Salads

Jungle Jumble (p. 49)

Tutti-Frutti Treat (p. 67)

Up and Down the Scales (p. 70)

Fruit juice gelatin (pp. 72-73)

Wheels, Whirls, and Curls (p. 84)

Tomato Torture Chamber (pp. 86-87)

Tic-Tac-Toe Fruit Combo (p. 88)

Four Seasons of Salads (pp. 100-1)

Birthday Banana Split (p. 104)

Happy Holiday Salad (p. 107)

Soups

Jack-O'-Lantern Soup (p. 106)

Breads

Ant Hills (p. 54)

Monkey Muffins (p. 55)

Main Courses

1 Potato, 2 Potato, 3 Potato, 4 (p. 68)

Pick Pockets (p. 80)

Pita Pizza (p. 81)

Scrambled Surprise (p. 90)

Skillet Skitters (p. 91)

Picnic Chicken Sticks (p. 92)

I Love Pizza (p. 96)

Hen on a Nest (p. 97)

Ham and Green Eggs (p. 98)

"My Hero" Sandwich (p. 99)

Desserts

Banana Blizzard (p. 53)

Ginger Bits (p. 69)

Birthday Banana Split (p. 104)

Frozen Fruit Snow (p. 105)

BRONCO BUSTER
BAKED POTATOES

Eat a baked potato anytime—breakfast, lunch, or dinner—they are great! They also are a delicious, filling snack.

---

4   medium   potatoes

---

1. Turn the oven on to 375°. Scrub the potatoes to remove all dirt. Dry.

2. Poke holes in each potato with a fork. Put the potatoes on a baking sheet and bake them at 375° for 1 hour or until thoroughly cooked. Use hotpads to remove the potatoes from the oven.

3. To serve, cut an "X" across the top and pull back the skin slightly. Keep leftover potatoes in the refrigerator to use in 1 Potato, 2 Potato, 3 Potato, 4 (p. 68) or Skillet Skitters (p. 91).

4. Top freely with chopped celery, chives, green peppers, or parsley.

Use any of the toppings listed on p. 113.

5. IDEA: You can bake 1 medium-sized potato in a microwave oven in 4 minutes. Wash it, poke holes in it with a fork, and bake it at full power for 2 minutes. Then turn the potato halfway around in the microwave and bake it for another 2 minutes at full power. Bake 2 potatoes for 8 minutes, 3 potatoes for 12 minutes, or 4 potatoes for 16 minutes.

Yield: 4 baked potatoes

	Cal	%Ft	P	F	C
Per Serving	145	1	4	T	33

TOPPINGS

Different toppings equal different tastes for your baked potato dinner. You can use more than one topping, too.

1/2 cup	plain yogurt, low-fat				
	Cal	**%Ft**	**P**	**F**	**C**
Per Serving	**62**	**31**	**4**	**2**	**6**
1/2 cup	cottage cheese, low-fat				
	Cal	**%Ft**	**P**	**F**	**C**
Per Serving	**90**	**10**	**14**	**1**	**4**
1/4 cup	salsa				
	Cal	**%Ft**	**P**	**F**	**C**
Per Serving	**16**	**T**	**1**	**T**	**4**
1/4 cup	Butter Buds®, liquid				
	Cal	**%Ft**	**P**	**F**	**C**
Per Serving	**24**	**T**	**0**	**0**	**2**
2 Tbl.	barbecue sauce				
	Cal	**%Ft**	**P**	**F**	**C**
Per Serving	**28**	**T**	**T**	**T**	**8**
1/2 cup	broccoli, cooked				
	Cal	**%Ft**	**P**	**F**	**C**
Per Serving	**35**	**T**	**4**	**T**	**6**
1/2 cup	favorite soup				
	Cal	**%Ft**	**P**	**F**	**C**
Per Serving	**150**	**5**	**8**	**1**	**15**
2 Tbl.	mozzarella cheese, shredded				
	Cal	**%Ft**	**P**	**F**	**C**
Per Serving	**45**	**60**	**5**	**3**	**T**
2 Tbl.	cheddar cheese, shredded				
	Cal	**%Ft**	**P**	**F**	**C**
Per Serving	**56**	**73**	**4**	**5**	**T**

Yield: 1 serving each

COWBOY-COWGIRL STIR-FRY

This stir-fry is as American as a cowboy or a cowgirl from the Old West.

1	cup	Rodeo Rice (p. 115)
1/2	cup	cooked lean hamburger
1	tsp.	oil (optional)
1	cup	frozen mixed vegetables
1	cup	frozen corn
10 3/4 -oz. can cream of mushroom soup		
1/2	cup	water

1. Cook rice (p. 115) and hamburger (p. 119). Set aside.

2. Measure out the water and set it aside. Open the can of soup and set it aside.

3. Turn the stove on to high (if you are using a frying pan) or heat up the nonstick electric wok to high. Spray the frying pan or wok with vegetable cooking spray (or pour in the oil). Add frozen mixed vegetables and frozen corn.

4. Cook the vegetables, stirring constantly with a long-handled wooden spoon for 4 minutes. Do not overcook them. They should be hot but still crisp.

5. Turn the heat to low. Add the water, cream of mushroom soup, and cooked hamburger. Stir until thoroughly mixed. Continue to cook, stirring constantly, for 2 minutes. Turn off the stove.

6. Serve 1/2 cup Cowboy-Cowgirl Stir-Fry over 1/4 cup Rodeo Rice. Ya hoo!

Yield: 4 (1/2-cup) servings

	Cal	%Ft	P	F	C
Per Serving	342	26	14	10	50

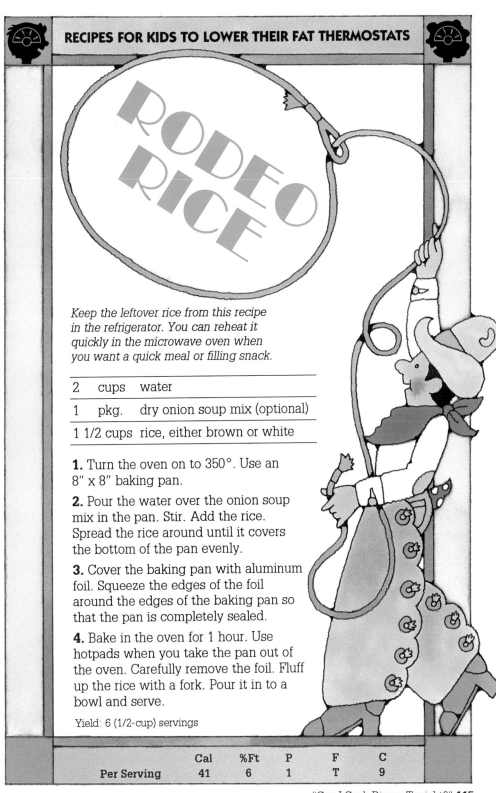

RODEO RICE

Keep the leftover rice from this recipe in the refrigerator. You can reheat it quickly in the microwave oven when you want a quick meal or filling snack.

2	cups	water
1	pkg.	dry onion soup mix (optional)
1 1/2	cups	rice, either brown or white

1. Turn the oven on to 350°. Use an 8" x 8" baking pan.

2. Pour the water over the onion soup mix in the pan. Stir. Add the rice. Spread the rice around until it covers the bottom of the pan evenly.

3. Cover the baking pan with aluminum foil. Squeeze the edges of the foil around the edges of the baking pan so that the pan is completely sealed.

4. Bake in the oven for 1 hour. Use hotpads when you take the pan out of the oven. Carefully remove the foil. Fluff up the rice with a fork. Pour it in to a bowl and serve.

Yield: 6 (1/2-cup) servings

	Cal	%Ft	P	F	C
Per Serving	41	6	1	T	9

WESTERN HOEDOWN
HAYSTACKS

Fill your plates and your stomachs with this low-fat meal.

1	cup	Rodeo Rice (p. 115)
1/2	cup	chicken, cooked
1	cup	water
1	tsp.	chicken bouillon granules
1	Tbl.	cornstarch
2	Tbl.	green onions, chopped
4	Tbl.	celery, thinly sliced
4	Tbl.	tomato, chopped
4	Tbl.	cheddar cheese, grated
4	Tbl.	crushed pineapple, drained
4	Tbl.	frozen peas
to taste		seasoning (p. 36)

1. COOK RICE: Make Rodeo Rice (p. 115). Set aside.

2. COOK CHICKEN: While the rice is cooking, have an adult help you skin and cook the chicken. When it is cooked, let it cool and pull the meat off the bones. Cut the meat into bite-sized pieces. Set aside.

3. COOK GRAVY: Do not turn on the stove yet. Pour the water in to a 1-quart saucepan. Whisk chicken bouillon granules and cornstarch into the water. Turn the stove on to medium-high. Stir the mixture constantly with a wooden spoon. As soon as it boils, it will thicken. Remove the pan from the heat. Turn off the stove. Set gravy aside.

4. Prepare the green onions, celery, tomatoes, cheese, crushed pineapple, frozen peas, rice, and chicken in separate containers.

5. Now "build a haystack." Put 1/4 cup hot rice on your plate. Add the toppings in the following order: 2 tablespoons chicken, 1/2 tablespoon green onions, 1 tablespoon each of celery, tomatoes, pineapple, peas, cheese, and 1/4 cup gravy. Enjoy!

Yield: 4 servings

	Cal	%Ft	P	F	C
Per Serving	221	16	11	4	35

SOMBRERO SALAD

You can heap this salad in the center of a warm tortilla so it looks like a sombrero.

1	corn tortilla
1/4 cup	cooked lean hamburger
1/2 cup	lettuce, washed and broken into pieces
1/2	tomato, chopped
2 Tbl.	low-fat mozzarella cheese, shredded
1 Tbl.	onion, chopped
to taste	salsa or catsup

1. COOK HAMBURGER (p. 119). Set aside 1/4 cup.

2. Prepare lettuce, tomatoes, onions, and salsa. Arrange each ingredient, including hamburger, in a separate container. Set aside.

3. Heat a corn tortilla in the microwave for 15 seconds on each side. Or, turn the oven on to 300°. Place a corn tortilla on a baking sheet and bake for 2 minutes. Turn. Cook for 2 more minutes. Take out the baking sheet and turn off the oven. Put the corn tortilla on a plate.

4. Build your sombrero salad in this order: a flat corn tortilla, hamburger, salsa or catsup, lettuce, tomatoes, onions, and cheese. Eat it with your fingers like a tostada.

Or fold the corn tortilla in half and eat like a taco. Olé!

5. IDEA: Replace the hamburger with 1/4 cup low-fat refried beans or with 1/4 cup cooked chicken.

Yield: 1 serving

	Cal	%Ft	P	F	C
Per Serving	284	34	49	11	16

SPAGHETTI

This is also tasty over cooked cauliflower.

10-oz. pkg.	alphabet pasta or curly noodles or spaghetti
3/4 cup	cooked lean hamburger
15-oz. can	tomato sauce
10 3/4-oz. can	tomato puree
1 Tbl.	Italian seasoning
1 Tbl.	beef bouillon granules

1. COOK HAMBURGER (p. 119): Measure out 3/4 cup hamburger. Set it aside. Put the rest of the hamburger in the refrigerator in a covered container.

2. COOK SAUCE: Do not turn the stove on yet. Into a 2-quart saucepan, pour tomato sauce and tomato puree. Stir. Turn the stove on to medium.

3. Add beef bouillon granules and Italian seasoning. Add hamburger. Stir. Turn heat to low. Simmer while you cook the pasta. Stir occasionally.

4. COOK PASTA: Into a large pan, pour 3 quarts of water. Turn stove on high and bring the water to a boil. Pour in a 10-oz. package of alphabet pasta, curly noodles, or spaghetti. Bring water back to a boil and cook uncovered for 8 to 10 minutes, stirring occasionally. Have an adult help you drain the pasta.

5. Serve 1/2 cup pasta immediately with 1/2 cup spaghetti sauce.

Yield: 6 (1-cup) servings

	Cal	%Ft	P	F	C
Per Serving	273	12	14	3	46

HOT-SHOT

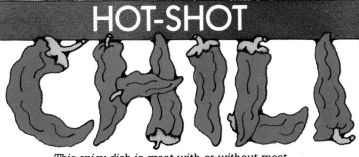

This spicy dish is great with or without meat.

1/2	cup	cooked lean hamburger
1	15-oz. can	kidney beans or chili beans
1	cup	stewed tomatoes with onions, celery, and green peppers, OR 1 cup tomato sauce
1/2	cup	tomato puree
1	Tbl.	beef bouillon granules
1	Tbl.	chili powder

1. COOK HAMBURGER: Turn the stove on to medium. Cook the hamburger in a medium frying pan, stirring occasionally with a long-handled wooden spoon until the meat is crumbly and brown. Turn off the stove. Pour the meat into a strainer and drain the grease from the meat in an empty can or bowl. Use a paper towel to blot off more grease. Measure out 1/2 cup hamburger. Set it aside. Put the rest of the hamburger in the refrigerator in a covered container.

2. COOK CHILI: Turn the stove back on to medium. Into a 2-quart saucepan, pour beans, stewed tomatoes, and tomato puree. Stir.

3. Add hamburger, beef bouillon granules, and chili powder. Stir.

4. Turn heat to low. Simmer for 5 minutes, stirring constantly. Serve hot. Like most bean recipes, this will taste better the second day.

Yield: 7 (1/2-cup) servings

5. IDEA: Pour 1/2 cup chili over a baked potato (p. 112).

6. IDEA: Pour 1/2 cup chili over 1/2 cup rice (p. 115).

	Cal	%Ft	P	F	C
Per Serving	**98**	**20**	**7**	**2**	**35**

"NO NEED TO KNEAD" BREAD

This bread has a heavy, moist texture with a wonderful, sweet taste. The best!

2	tsp.	honey
2 2/3 cups		lukewarm water
4	tsp.	dry yeast
3	Tbl.	honey
5	cups	whole wheat flour
1/2	tsp.	salt
1/4	cup	wheat germ
1	Tbl.	sesame seeds (optional)

1. Turn the oven on to 400°. In a medium bowl, stir 2 teaspoons honey in 2/3 cup lukewarm water. Make sure the water is only lukewarm; if it is too hot, it will kill the yeast. Sprinkle the yeast over the honey and water mixture. Set aside for 10 minutes. (The yeast will begin to grow and make the water cloudy and foamy.)

2. While the yeast is growing, combine 3 tablespoons honey with 2/3 cup lukewarm water in another bowl. Pour it in with the yeast mixture. Set aside.

3. Place the flour in a large bowl. Add salt and wheat germ. Stir. Then add 1 1/3 cups lukewarm water and the yeast mixture. Stir with a strong spoon until completely mixed. Dough will be sticky. Set aside.

4. Spray two loaf pans with vegetable cooking spray. Divide the dough in half and spoon each half in to a loaf pan. Use the spoon to press the dough evenly in the pan. Use a wet spatula to smooth the rough spots off the top of the dough. Sprinkle sesame seeds over the top of the loaf, if desired. Allow the dough to rise a little higher than the top of the pan.

5. Bake the bread for 30 minutes. Use hotpads to take the pans out of the oven. Set the pans on a rack to cool for 10 minutes. Then turn the bread out of the pans. Slice and enjoy warm bread!

Yield: 2 loaves; each loaf = 16 (1/2-inch) slices

	Cal	%Ft	P	F	C
Per Slice	148	6	6	1	32

BREAD MACHINES

A loaf of this delicious bread makes a nice gift for your friends.

Baking bread is easy with a bread machine. All you have to do is measure the ingredients carefully, pour them into the bread machine, and start it. The bread machine will mix the dough, knead it, let it rise, and bake it. Bread is filling and nutritious. A bread machine puts many kinds of bread at your fingertips for snacks or toast. Orange bread, applesauce cinnamon bread, banana bread, carrot bread, vegetable juice bread, and raisin bread are only a few of the kinds of bread you can bake yourself. Eat a slice of bread with chili or soup or just a glass of milk. Or cover a slice of bread with Jam Session (p. 60) or another all-fruit jam (available at the grocery store).

You can buy a bread machine at most large chain department stores. A recipe book will come with your bread machine. You can also find recipe books in bookstores or libraries. Look for recipes that focus on using whole grains and natural sweeteners. Have fun!

Whole Wheat Honey Bread

	Small Loaf	Medium Loaf	Large Loaf
water	3/4 cup	1 1/8 cups	1 1/2 cups
honey	3 Tbl.	1/4 cup	1/3 cup
salt	1/4 tsp.	1/3 tsp.	1/2 tsp.
whole wheat flour	1 cup	1 1/2 cups	2 cups
bread flour	1 cup	1 1/2 cups	2 cups
yeast	2 tsp.	2 1/2 tsp.	3 tsp.

	Cal	%Ft	P	F	C
Per 1/2-inch slice	103	3	3	T	22

APPLE-TUNA TOSS

This is a refreshing combination of fruit and tuna in a tossed salad.

1. Make Orange Dip. Set aside.

2. In a large bowl, toss lettuce, apples, tuna, and oranges together. Set bowl aside.

3. Serve salad on a plate. Pour Orange Dip over salad. Store leftover salad in the refrigerator in a covered container.

4. IDEA: For a change, replace the tuna with chicken and replace the orange pieces with 1 cup crushed pineapple.

5. IDEA: Here's an idea for a salad that can be eaten for lunch or used to fill a pocket sandwich (Pick Pockets, p. 80).

2	cups	lettuce, washed and broken into pieces
1	cup	red apples, not peeled, chopped
3 1/4-oz. can		water-packed tuna, drained
1		orange, peeled and sectioned
1/4	cup	Orange Dip (p. 89)

Yield: 4 (1-cup) servings

	Cal	%Ft	P	F	C
Per Serving	107	9	9	1	17

TIPS
FOR PARENTS
PART 3

TIPS FOR MOM AND DAD

This chapter is to help parents in four areas: first, to encourage their children as they learn to lower their fat thermostats; second, to review basic nutrition; third, help their children become more active physically; and fourth, to give parents a glimpse into some of the literature covering childhood obesity.

Children have three important selves: self-worth, self-esteem, and self-confidence. Following is a summary of each.

Self-Worth

Just as Hippocrates told his medical students to "do no harm" to their patients, parents need to be careful to do no harm to their children. At birth, children have a priceless possession: self-worth. They believe they are worthwhile in and of themselves, and that this value is not related in any way to their performance.

Since it is the parents who help children maintain their feelings of self-worth, they need to make sure they don't do anything that diminishes it. Angry looks, words, and actions can destroy some children's feelings of self-worth. Refusing to listen to children can make them feel unimportant.

Neglect and abuse take a tremendous toll on how children feel. By the time children enter the third grade, they may be plagued with self-doubt. This can make them subject to psychological and physical illness and raise their fat thermostat setting. Parents need to do things continually that show children that they are loved and important.

Self-Esteem

Unlike self-worth, self-esteem is not present at birth but develops as children do something that is delightful to others. The first smile, the first word, the first step all help children's self-esteem grow as parents react to them.

Until about eight years of age, children see themselves as either

Encourage your children.

competent or incompetent in doing a specific thing.[1] Although being overweight may hamper their ability to do certain tasks, they may not be self-conscious about the obesity itself. Parents may be tempted to tell children that they need to diet, but they shouldn't. Children will simply feel that they are not good.[2]

In the preteen years, overweight children become increasingly aware that their physical proportions are a disadvantage. Often, other children will tease them. This impaired self-esteem because of physical appearance may continue into adulthood. When under stress, these children may resort to eating to escape the pain of not feeling physically acceptable. The long-term consequences are greater weight gain and decreased self-esteem. Even if children get good grades and are accomplished in many other ways, they will still feel that they are not valuable. Parents need to make a point of giving children credit for specific things that they do. Parents should not expect perfection because that teaches children that they are not valuable unless they are perfect.

Self-Confidence

As children mature, they need to develop a sense that they can

Figure 1

SOME WAYS TO GIVE YOUR CHILD CREDIT

Frequently give your child a big smile, a hug, or a kiss.

Sincerely tell your child :

Outstanding - I Knew You Could Do It - I'm Proud of You - You Mean A Lot to Me - How Smart - Way to Go - Well Done - Good Job - You're Beautiful - Excellent - You're Really Special - Nice Work - You're a Winner - I Like You - You've Discovered the Secret - You Learned It Right - You Brighten My Day - You Are Fun - You're Wonderful - You Made My Day - You're Precious - That's Exciting - Keep Up the Good Work - You're Growing Up - I Respect You - That's Right - Good For You - Thanks For Sharing - Super - That's Incredible - Fantastic - You're Important to Me - You Worked Hard - I Like the Way You Listened - Beautiful - You're a Good Friend - I Love You - Great Discovery - Spectacular - I Trust You - Awesome - I Love Your Humor - You're Incredible - Fantastic - Terrific - You Belong do many things. Parents become teachers that encourage children to explore the world around them. If children have experience solving problems or mastering skills, they will be better able to face new situations.

Self Questions

Whenever parents do something that directly affects their children they need to ask themselves, "Will I help my child's feelings of self-worth and self-esteem? Will I help increase my child's self-confidence?" Parents need to be very careful so they will not impair a precious part of a child's self-systems. Parents need to actively plan ways of promoting children's self-worth, self-esteem, and self-confidence. Figure 1 has some examples of things parents can say and do to encourage a child's self. Parents can complete Figure 2 to plan specific things they can do.

Self-Control

Our experience with overweight adults is that they have great self-control part of the time. How else could they go on starvation diets for months on end? But once they lose self-control, they often give up and say, "I've blown it! I might as well eat all I want." This "black and white" thinking typically results in periods of overeating and rapid weight gain. Parents don't expect an infant to exercise self-control, but they do begin to expect it by the time children pass through the "terrible twos."

The development of a child's self-control comes largely from observations of parents and older siblings.[3] Some authorities believe

Figure 2

THINGS I WILL DO TO BUILD MY CHILD'S SELF

that overweight children with poor self-control are more likely to have parents who have problems delaying gratification, especially when it comes to what they eat.[4] Parents may want to take a look at themselves and other family members and ask what kind of examples they have been for their children. Parents don't have to have perfect self-control. In fact, children need to see parents dealing with stressful situations and perhaps even becoming upset. Children need to know that it is natural to have challenges but that they should seek real solutions rather than burying the pain in cookies and malted milk shakes.

Stress

How parents choose to raise their children has a significant effect on a child's ability to make good decisions. To grow into competent adults, children need experience in making good decisions while in the protective environment of the home. Parents who rigidly establish narrow rules of acceptable behavior often find that when their children go outside immediate supervision, they fail to make good decisions. How can children develop internal guidelines when the external ones are so tight? This seems to be particularly true of food choices. Children may become covert in their behavior, even within the home. They may manipulate others to obtain food for them or find ways to stash food and consume it when no one is

around. Children may tend to do more covert eating as they become older if they have not developed inner values to help them make better eating choices.

One child-rearing style that seems to be effective in helping children develop internal values is called "person-oriented" reasoning.[5, 6] This style emphasizes the consequences of a child's behavior on self, friends, and other important people rather than stressing rules of conduct made by parents. As children develop stronger internal values, they become more self-governing and will make better decisions regarding eating.

From the diagram on page xii, parents can learn the many factors that can cause the fat thermostat setting to go up. The first stress most children experience comes from within the family. Often parents are unaware of the consequences their decisions have on their children. One study found that mothers who feel independent tend to feed their children healthier foods.[7] It is also likely that when mothers

Relax, and be happy!

have healthy dietary habits, they feel better and function more independently. This attitude is healthier for their children.

Parents also need to look at their own feelings of satisfaction in their own lives. They may want to follow these suggestions: Take 15 minutes 3 or 4 times a week. Find a pleasant place. Put on some relaxing music. Dim the lights. Let your mind wander to matters that trouble you. It sometimes helps to make a list of concerns. Choose the most pressing problem. Use the steps for Effective Problem-Solving listed in Figure 3. Discuss possible solutions with your spouse, a good friend, or a religious or other adviser. Develop some promising solutions. Put the plan into action.

Figure 3
STEPS FOR EFFECTIVE PROBLEM-SOLVING

1. Describe the problem _____

_____

2. How is this your problem? _____

_____

3. What will be different for you when the problem is solved? _____

_____

4. Brainstorm as many solutions as you can _____

_____

_____

_____

_____

5. Pick the best solution _____

_____

6. Date you will evaluate results _____

7. Results _____

_____

If results are not satisfactory, recycle through above 7 steps.

As you resolve the issue, consider sharing your experience with your child, who may profit from your healthy example.

Conflict within the home can increase the fat thermostat settings in parents and in their children.[8] It also affects their physical health. Parents and children often weigh more in families where the members do not express feelings freely.[9] Parents need to work for emotional cohesiveness and honest expression in their families. Further, it has been found that mothers who are depressed tend to have heavier children than nondepressed mothers.[10]

Parent-Child Interactions

Parents need to look at how they interact with children regarding food and physical activity. Studies have shown some interesting, although not surprising, results. When parents encourage children to be active, children are more likely to be active. If parents encourage children to be inactive, children

Play with your children.

are more likely to be sedentary.[11] Another study showed that parents who themselves were overweight tended to not encourage their children to be physically active.[12] The researchers also found that the more parents encouraged children to eat, the less children were encouraged to be physically active.

Research shows that the intake of food by overweight adults is less than or about the same as that of normal-weight adults.[13] One of the better studies of childhood obesity showed no relationship between the amount that was eaten and the degree of adiposity in the child.[14] In another intriguing study the researchers found that obese boys ate much faster, were served larger and more frequent portions by their mothers, and ate more than their normal-weight brothers and peers.[15] This study is one of the few that showed the overweight child eating more than the normal-weight child. One researcher concluded that in pediatric obesity, food intake might help explain why some children become overweight and their siblings do not.[16] Under routine conditions children probably don't overeat but may have short periods of time when they binge. These would probably not be reported in many studies because they are done in private and children may not remember them.

When families eat together, parents need to notice if there are

Nurse your baby.

differences in how overweight children eat compared to their normal-weight siblings. Do they tend to eat faster and make verbal or nonverbal requests for seconds? Are they given or do they take larger servings? Do they savor their food or rapidly swallow it almost without chewing? As a parent, do you have inner thoughts that you need to make sure your overweight children have enough food? Do you automatically give them second servings even if they don't ask for them? As a minimum you need to give them the opportunity to request more food. If you usually put the food on your children's plates, be sure not to give your overweight children more than the others.

You may notice some negative response from them as you begin to make these changes. That's okay. It tells you that you are changing the unspoken contract with them regarding how you do meals. Discuss their feelings with them in private. See if they can come up with ways of eating that

will better fit into the healthy fat thermostat guidelines.

Infant Nutrition

Most fat cells are created during the first year of life. Often those who are overweight as adults started this process in their first year. Researchers have noticed that some babies have a voracious eating style. They drink faster and want to eat more frequently. Bottle-fed babies typically consume more than breast-fed babies.[17] They also tend to eat solid foods earlier and put on weight faster.[18] British infants ate significantly more than Swedish infants and showed twice as much overweight.[19] Interestingly, thin babies don't like sweeteners added to their formula, while medium-weight to overweight babies often prefer sweet-tasting fluids.[20]

Scientists have found that humans have an innate preference for sweets and avoid bitter-tasting substances.[21] All other taste preferences are learned. If babies eat something noxious and become nauseated shortly afterwards, they probably will avoid that taste in the future. Studies with rats show that when tastes are paired with unwholesome events, the animal will avoid that taste. If children see parents make a face of disgust when they put something in their mouths they, too, will eventually avoid that taste. If children see parents smiling when they eat something, they likely will learn to like that flavor. And as children grow older, they will also notice what other children like. This is why food manufacturers advertise so much on television. They want to shape children's preferences toward their products. In 1993 the National Cancer Institute spent $400,000 to encourage people to eat more vegetables and fruits. In 1992, a cereal company spent $34,000,000 promoting one of their products.[22] Parents can see that unless they take an active part in helping children develop preferences for healthier and slimming foods, they will follow the American-eating rut of fats, sugar, and junk foods.

Mothers can help infants become normal-weight adults by breast-feeding them.* As in adults, more frequent eating of smaller amounts seems to develop thinner babies.[23] Less frequent, larger meals tends to make them fatter. If mothers must bottle-feed their babies, they should learn to recognize what their babies do when they are full. Parents shouldn't give babies the rest of the bottle, even if there is only one ounce left. If babies are fussing, mothers need to find other activities that can stimulate the baby but don't involve eating. When the parent is relaxed at feeding time, the baby may tend to be a more relaxed and contented child. Even if babies seem overweight, that doesn't mean they will become overweight adults. About two-thirds of overweight babies become normal-weight adults.[24]

While babies show a steep gain in fatness during their first year, they become significantly leaner during the next two years. By the fourth year, those who end up being obese begin to store fat more rapidly than their peers.[25] Parents need to be aware of this important phase and help children remain at a normal weight.

Parents need to look at their own eating habits. They need to learn to like vegetables, eat a wide variety of foods, and limit fats and sugars. Even if parents have no significant weight problem, this style of food selection will be very healthy for them and their whole family. Many families have gone from whole milk to 2% fat milk to 1% fat or skim milk with relative ease. Children born into families who

Eat more vegetables.

*There is an added benefit to mothers who breast-feed their children. A recent study found that mothers who breast-fed for from four months to one year had an 11 percent lower risk of breast cancer. Those who breast-fed for at least two years over the course of their life had a 25 percent lower risk of breast cancer. *(New England Journal of Medicine*, 330:81, 1994, as reported in *Nutrition Action Health Letter*, 21, no. 2, p. 4, 1994.)

drink skim milk typically find whole or even 2% fat milk distasteful.

Some parents attempt to get children to eat vegetables by rewarding them with money. While this sometimes works for the short term, it is not a good way to help children make good food choices. They often end up disliking the food they were rewarded for eating and discontinue eating it when the reward is no longer given.[26] Children are more motivated by the internal sensation of the good taste than by what they will gain by eating the food. So if parents want their children to eat vegetables and other healthy, low-fat foods, they need to eat and enjoy them themselves.

Similarly, the best way for children to learn to exercise regularly is to see parents enjoying aerobic activities.

There is concern in the scientific community that parents may cause more damage to their children when they overly emphasize obesity and bad food, such as sugar, than if they take a more relaxed, positive attitude toward food intake.[27] Using guilt to force children to diet can lead to failure, self-hatred, and rebound binge eating, and can be the start of an eating disorder.

Some have theorized[28] that young girls who feel they have not gotten enough parental care may engage in care-giving to help compensate. They may feed and take care of younger brothers and sisters. They may also attempt to fill this need by overeating. Food can act as a universal tranquilizer which helps children feel better in the short term. In the long term they can develop an addiction-like dependency on overeating. In addition, the tranquilized body tends to be inactive and docile, almost as if it were in a minor form of hibernation. As the body lowers its metabolic rate, the problem of the excess intake of calories increases the storage of fat. Overeating might also cause a release of dopamine in the brain, which can decrease the desire for physical activity.

Earlier research is now being reexamined. Obesity was often used as the dependent variable by naive researchers who assumed that to lose weight all one had to do was decrease calories-in and increase exercise or calories-out. By classifying their participants as either obese or normal they were unable to find any differences in the amount of food they consumed.[29] Most overweight people want to be thinner. If they aren't familiar with the factors

Eat less fats and sugars.

that raise the fat thermostat setting, they often diet or restrict calories. They lose weight and keep it off for a while, then they "go off their diet" and over-consume foods as they regain weight. This has been called the "yo-yo" cycle.

If one overweight person is on a 1,200-calorie diet and another of the same weight is not dieting and eating 2,800 calories, we would conclude that they ate the same amount as a normal-weight woman eating 2,000 calories. One study did show this.[30] Nondieting overweight adults ate significantly more food than nondieting, normal-weight subjects. Dieting overweight adults ate significantly less food than those who were normal weight.

We can't say that the same is true for overweight children because we are unaware of any study that substantiates this fact. However, children are beginning to diet at earlier ages and probably are unable to control the rebound long-term hunger which results. So the problem with "yo-yo" dieting needs to be addressed in children as well as adults. In children the binges may be equally responsible for weight gain. This can lead to rapid weight gain if the binging occurs too frequently.[31]

Physical Activities

Long-range weight control appears optimal when overweight children learn to control their own eating behaviors and physical activities rather than have parents

completely take over the project.[32] However, parents can make fun activities part of daily living. Go for walks with your children for fun. Take a nature hike and learn about the plants that you find. Make a rock collection from the stones children find as they walk with you. Find some interesting bike trails near your home and have a family bike day. Children will not only benefit from the exercise; they will also be away from food during that time.

Parental emphasis needs to be on enduring changes in behaviors that will lower the fat thermostat setting. It isn't always necessary to set up structured aerobic exercise sessions for children; modifying normal activities so they are more physically intensive has been shown to have better long-term results.[33]

Look for ways you can encourage your children to walk more or climb more stairs without making them feel that "they are exercising"[34] As children become more comfortable with the increased level of physical activity, they may become more receptive to beginning aerobic exercises at least three times a week.

A study involving more than 8,000 adolescents throughout the United States found that there is a minimum level of physical activity that is required for children to not be severely overweight.[35] The more sedentary children are, the more overweight they are.[36] The least fit were the most overweight and seemed to benefit most from increased levels of physical activity.[37]

On the other hand, there is significant information showing that overweight children are less physically active than other children.[38, 39, 40] For example, in the same study that found overweight boys ate more than their normal-weight brothers, it was concluded that they were far less active inside their homes although they were about as active at school.[41] Observations made at public places where stairs and escalators were side by side found that normal-weight children chose the stairs two to four times more frequently than the overweight children.[42]

Although little research has been done on the biases in reporting physical activity, one researcher observed that overweight subjects tend to be more physically active when they are being studied.[43] Perhaps they are so sensitive to their physical appearance they work extra hard

to appear active if they know they are being monitored. When they no longer believe they are being watched they slip back into a less-active state.

Genes

A recent study in Denmark shows that adopted children more closely resembled their birth parents than their adopted parents.[44] While this and other studies confirm the importance of the genetic and biochemical components of energy stored as body fat, it does not mean that the environment plays no role. There is much parents can do to influence children's food and activity choices that can keep their fat thermostat set at a lower range.

While the genes do play a role in how high a child's fat thermostat setting is at first, the way a child deals with his or her environment has much to do with how fat he or she becomes.[45] In fact, there is no single cause of obesity. To help children lower their fat thermostat setting, parents will need to help them control factors within themselves, elements within the family, and interactions among peers.[46] Parents are in the best position to influence the eating behaviors and physical activities of children.[47] As parents wisely teach these concepts and live them, their children can achieve healthy, active bodies that will serve them well throughout their lives.

EATING DISORDERS

Janet is a 35-year-old woman who has been bulimic for fifteen years. Her story is typical. In high school, she was beautiful, athletic, and a straight-A student. But she was always on a diet and soon became anorexic. Sometimes she would go for days eating nothing but candy bars and diet sodas. She felt a lack of self-control and guilt when she ate anything. When her self-imposed starvation became impossible to continue, she began to binge and purge.

Today, she has no close friends and regrets dropping out of college. Her hair is thin and her face is gaunt. She has little energy and is continually in a state of depression. She has suffered various medical problems, including tooth decay and broken ribs from self-induced vomiting. Even on her best days she looks unhealthy.

About dinner time, Janet begins eating while watching television or reading the newspaper. She eats until she can hold no more. Then she gets rid of it and eats again. She continues this binge-purge cycle until the early morning hours when she collapses on her bed in utter exhaustion.

The next day, almost every waking hour is spent thinking and preparing for the high point of her day—binging and purging. She has no real goals outside of those required to maintain her bulimia. From time to time she becomes so weak that she has to be hospitalized. She is always perfectly compliant. Promptly after she is discharged from the hospital, she goes back to her binging and purging. She seems to take some satisfaction knowing that the best professionals have not cured her.

The Fear of Fatness

The fear of becoming fat is at the heart of anorexia nervosa and bulimia nervosa. There are thousands of cues in today's society which say "You can't be too thin or too rich." Almost all the idols of teenagers are very thin. Even a slender girl without

Eating disorders begin between the ages of 12 and 25.

tendencies toward anorexia could easily believe she is fat when she compares herself to certain movie or television stars. Those girls with a tendency toward anorexia will distort reality to such an extreme that they see themselves as fat even if they are the same size as the movie or television star.

Some professionals classify eating disorders as obesity, anorexia nervosa, and bulimia nervosa.[1] Others include only anorexia and bulimia because they have greater short-term health risks.

Anorexia Nervosa

Girls as young as eight years old may try severe dieting, but true anorexia usually begins between the ages of 12 and 25, although a 70-year-old woman was recently diagnosed with anorexia.[2] About 1 percent of young women get anorexia, and from 5 to 18 percent of them die from it. Boys or young men rarely suffer from anorexia, and only 5 to 10 percent of bulimics are male.

Anorexia is often triggered by

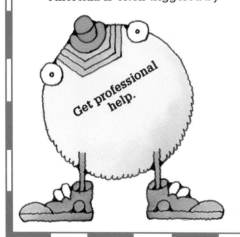

Get professional help.

a remark from someone who is important to a child. Some girls remember feeling fat when boys at school teased them about their appearance. Others remember their mom or dad implying or actually saying to them that they were too fat. Some children don't even remember when they first started feeling fat.

For girls, perhaps it is more than coincidental that eating disorders begin after they enter puberty. Some girls are not ready for the change from the comfortable flat angles of childhood to the curves of womanhood. Others may be overwhelmed by the potential responsibilities of motherhood so they either consciously or unconsciously become so thin that they no longer have menstrual periods. Victims of physical abuse, sexual abuse, or other traumas often experience profound forms of eating disorders. For some young women, anorexia is simply an attempt to exert self-control in a setting of unmanageable chaos where too much is expected of them.

Whatever the cause, the typical young woman with anorexia rarely expresses any negative emotions or causes problems, so parents often think everything is fine. However, the young woman may be exhibiting the nearly imperceptible signs of an eating disorder. Her body weight may be below 85 percent of her normal weight. At mealtime, she may quietly withdraw and become secretive. She may say she isn't hungry or that she ate before she came home. If she does eat a meal with the family, she may excuse herself quickly, go to the bathroom, and vomit.

Anorexia causes a great deal of physical discomfort because the fat thermostat setpoint is much higher than the actual weight. Instead of developing self-control, self-starvation causes the body to behave as if it were in a famine and it begins to produce chemicals that make it a fat-storer rather than a fat-burner. The elevated setpoint lowers metabolism, causes fatigue, and increases hunger. The fat thermostat setting goes up in order to survive even as the body weight goes down. These young women eventually begin to feel depressed and weak. Their thoughts become centered on food. They even begin to fantasize about it, but never actually eat because of their fear of becoming fat.

Bulimia Nervosa

Bulimia began to be identified in the 1960s as a variation of anorexia. Both conditions require the victim to have a fear of gaining weight and a powerful concern about body shape. About 10 percent of girls who become bulimic start out with anorexia. Anorectics rarely acknowledge having a problem, but bulimics know that something is wrong. They admit that their behavior is abnormal—even bizarre.

Bulimia is usually triggered by the powerful hunger drives experienced when body weight is below the fat thermostat setpoint weight. Those with bulimia feel out of control as soon as they have anything to eat. They feel overwhelmed by the fear of fatness, especially when they can't stop eating. They eat much more than they planned, and then they feel trapped because they believe that the food will make them fat. The only thing that relieves their fear is knowing that they can throw up the food, even though they feel sick when they force themselves to vomit.

With bulimia there are repeated periods of binge eating over which the victim has little control. There is a persistent focus on body shape and weight even if the person is under his or her ideal body weight. Although self-induced vomiting is the most common way those with bulimia compensate for the large amounts of food they eat, they may also abuse laxatives, diuretics, and enemas. They may completely avoid food for days on end. Some will compulsively exercise. A few will chew but not swallow the food.

Perhaps the most tragic consequence of bulimia is that it becomes addictive. For bulimics, the experience of filling the stomach to the point of pain then finding almost instant relief when they vomit has a bittersweet riveting power. Energy declines, school work is left undone, and friendships fade away, but nothing is as satisfying to them as the binge followed by the purge.

Although the children who become bulimic are often very successful at school, they are still dependent on their families. Typically, they are intelligent, attractive young women who could have successful careers. Their professed goal in life is to marry and have children. Not only are they happy to be female, they tend to be overly feminine. They want to be perfect and, to them, that means having an ultrathin body. The focus on thinness makes them continually compare themselves to other young women. Their self-image distortions make them feel fatter and less successful than others.

Hoarding Food

As the binge-purge cycles become habitual, the events take more and more time. At first bulimics vomit only once in a while and continue their regular activities. Then it dawns on them that they have discovered a "great secret"—they can control their weight through vomiting. So they eat more and almost always throw it up. The binge-purge events become more frequent and crowd out other important activities. Much of their available money is spent on food. They take large amounts of food from the family's supply, then deny taking the food. Soon they begin to feel like liars. They lose the feeling of inner joy and satisfaction that comes with real achievement.

Many of those with bulimia choose junk foods for their binges. They may hoard food until there is no more room to hide it. A bulimic can eat anywhere from 1,000 to 20,000 calories during a binge. A bulimic girl can eat 5 to 10 times the amount of food a normal woman eats in a day. This obviously requires careful scheming for anyone living in a family. Because those with bulimia feel forced to hide their behavior, they are often filled with shame. They feel isolated and lonely. Their obsession with food contributes to their low self-esteem.

Watch for the subtle signs of anorexia and bulimia.

Listen to your children

The Big Secret

Vomiting is the "big secret" for those with bulimia. Bulimics may overeat with their friends and may even admit to vomiting. However, it is extremely rare for them to purge when others are present. They go to great lengths to avoid detection, such as turning on the shower to cover the sounds of regurgitation. They choose a time when they can be alone to overeat and then purge.

Bulimics sometimes fall into the dangerous habit of using an emetic, such as Ipecac syrup, to produce vomiting. This can sometimes cause such violent contractions in a full stomach that it tears the stomach lining. But those with bulimia are so driven by the need to completely empty the stomach that they often take massive doses of the emetic. Some even end up in the emergency room of a hospital. If vomiting does not follow use of the Ipecac syrup, it may be absorbed into the body and can lead to serious and even fatal heart disease. Parents who think their child may be abusing Ipecac need to take precautions quickly to stop it.

Avoiding Feelings

Almost all people with an eating disorder admit it helps them to avoid their own feelings. Those with anorexia experience a numbing of their feelings. Those with bulimia feel "clean" or "safe" after they purge. Both deal with their problems in the privacy of their own bedroom or bathroom. Typically, they don't have the energy to directly confront their everyday problems. When they are disappointed, they feel helpless instead of becoming angry.

For those with bulimia, anger can be the emotion that gives them a sense of dignity and helps them overcome their eating disorder. Typically, those with eating disorders learned as children to be openly submissive and nonassertive. Just the thought of becoming angry was probably disconcerting for them and would cause them to lose control. They learned that openly acting out their negative feelings not only drew unwanted attention to them but threatened the stability of their dependent relationships. They lacked the confidence of knowing that they could manage all by themselves. They endured abuse rather than standing up for themselves. Because they learned to hide their feelings, they didn't learn how to genuinely show their emotions. Even when they thought they had expressed anger, others may have had no clue that they were angry.

How Parents Can Help

Children with an eating disorder focus on their feelings while parents focus on the eating disorder. Those with an eating disorder need to learn to focus on their behavior in order to overcome their compulsion, and parents need to gain an understanding of how the child is feeling. Parents cannot force children to change. No matter how powerful the parents are, the child will remain unchanged inside even though he or she may appear to change for the parent. There is an old saying among therapists, "You can't want people to get better more than they want it." By understanding the child's feelings, parents may begin to understand the behaviors. Giving up an eating disorder is a process rather than a single event. The earlier the problem is recognized, the easier it is to deal with. The problem is rarely a simple lack of self-control. The source of the problem is deep within the child's experience and can be understood and remedied in an atmosphere of acceptance and love. Because parents are an integral part of the environment in which the behaviors are developed, they can be an important part of helping the child achieve a more effective way of dealing with life.

Figure 4 is a chart of various body types that is sometimes used when treating young women with eating disorders. It is most often used in a group setting. Each young woman is asked to decide the body type of each of

Figure 4
HOW DO YOU PICTURE YOURSELF?

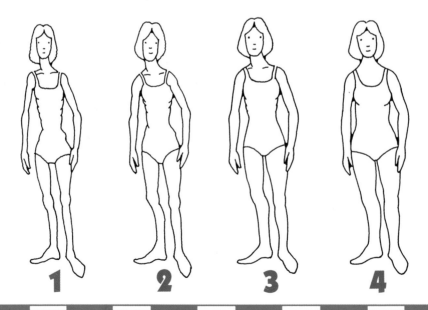

the other young women in the group. Then they are asked to rate their own body type. Typically all young women in the group agree on the body type of each of the other young women in the group, but each rates herself two or more body types fatter than the others rated her.

Parents can use this chart to see how their daughter rates her own body type. If the daughter's view is distorted, she may be a potential victim of eating disorders.

Also, this chart provides parents with an opportunity to discuss eating disorders with their daughter. Usually those with eating disorders are reluctant to accept the opinions of others regarding their body size. If the daughter accepts her parents' feedback, she may not be struggling with an eating disorder.

But if she frankly denies the parents' belief or becomes upset, she may have an eating disorder. Parents shouldn't expect her to be concerned about her emaciated appearance because she may take great pride in it. She will not acknowledge a problem even if she is actually near death from starvation. However, she may respond to her parents listening to her feelings.

As part of the discussion resulting from the use of the above chart, parents can take time to discuss how the fat thermostat operates. Parents can use the diagram of the fat thermostat mechanism on page xii. This chart shows the power of the fat thermostat. Parents can remind children that the goal is to lower the setpoint. Stress, including dieting and starvation, raises the setpoint. Eating

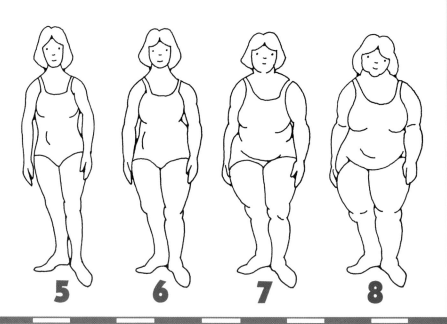

Consider your child's viewpoint.

adequate amounts of healthy complex carbohydrates helps relax it, and moderate exercise will lower it. By mastering these concepts, children will rarely be bothered by eating disorders. They will live a life in harmony with their fat thermostat which is set at a good weight for them.

Getting Professional Help

Dealing with children with an eating disorder is a complex challenge. If a child is more than 20 percent under his or her ideal weight, parents should consult a psychologist, medical doctor, or other expert who has experience treating eating disorders. A professional who also understands the way the fat thermostat works would be especially helpful. Parents should be willing to participate in the therapy and to change any family habits that may be contributing to the problem. They need to remain open as therapy progresses but to not become totally preoccupied with the child's eating disorder.[3] Parents need to show faith that

the eating disorder can be overcome.

Helping children with an eating disorder find humor and pleasure can be a step in the right direction. These children are in so much pain that their view of life is very serious. Parents can set a good example by expressing humor in their own lives, admitting to mistakes, and not taking things too seriously. Perhaps parents can share the concerns they had about their own weight when they were teenagers. Using "I" statements works better than "you" statements, which immediately put children on the defensive. Remember that children with eating disorders won't find anything that is said about their body even remotely funny and they hate to be nagged. Parents need to do things that build feelings of self-worth, self-esteem, and self-confidence.

Parents must be very careful not to violate any trust their children place in them. Usually the problem is the way children perceive their parents' expectations and not the parents' actual expectations. Most parents do not demand that their children be perfect. Still, parents need to consider their child's point of view.

Dad, does your daughter idolize you? Are you preoccupied and so involved in your own life that there is little time for her? Are you so stressed by life that your daughter fears adding another burden, herself and her problems, to your already overloaded schedule? Is there something that you can do to change this? Not only will you be healthier if you say "no" to excessive demands from work, but you will enjoy some one-on-one time with your daughter. Keep these times relaxed and let them be a chance to really listen to her. You don't need an agenda. Sometimes it is fine to just be together, even if nothing is said. As she learns that you care enough to take time with her, she may begin to share her deepest feelings. Listening without judging gives her hope that she can come out of her isolation.

Mom, you also have the wonderful opportunity of listening to your daughter. Find as many times and ways as you can to hear what your child says and, more importantly, feels. She doesn't need solutions or advice. She needs unconditional love. You may have to keep quiet when what she does is inappropriate. While dads are sometimes inclined toward harsh judgment, moms may be inclined toward softening the consequences of their daughter's eating disorder. This can make her feel trapped and incompetent.

Don't say, "I told you so" when she is pouring out her heart to you. Be grateful that she is beginning to leave her world of secrecy. Simple attentive silence will encourage her to tell you more. As you begin to understand her painful emotions, say something like "You must feel very lonely" or "You seem so afraid of becoming fat." Younger children may find it easier to talk. Older teenagers may feel embarrassed to share their feelings. Please be persistent in listening. Don't lecture or say "Why did you do that?" It will make your daughter feel defensive. Ask "what were you feeling when you did that?" It may help her understand the feelings that preceded the behavior. Be patient as she struggles to understand her feelings. You may hear things like, "I have never told this to anyone before" or "You really seem to understand." When you hear this, you may be assured that your daughter's big secret is less shameful for her and that she is on the path to recovery.

Endnotes for this chapter are available by telephoning 1-800-748-5100 or by sending a self-addressed, stamped envelope to Vitality House International, Inc., 1675 N. Freedom Blvd., #11-C, Provo, UT 84604-2570.

THE BALANCING ACT GAME

"LET'S EAT"

"LET'S PLAY"

"YES, I CAN"

START
Draw 1 "Let's Play" card when you pass this space.
Draw 2 "Let's Play" cards when you land on this space.

SWEET TOOTH
Return 1 "Let's Eat" card.

COMPLEX CARBO-HYDRATES
"LET'S EAT"
Draw 1 Complex CARBOHYDRATE card.

COUCH POTATO
"LET'S EAT"
Return 1 "Let's Play" card.

FRUIT
Draw 1 FRUIT card.

"I'M THIRSTY"
Draw 1 "Let's Play" card and 1 "Let's Eat" card.

LOW-FAT DAIRY
"LET'S EAT"
Draw 1 Low-Fat DAIRY card.

SWEET TOOTH
Return 1 "Let's Eat" card.

PROTEIN
"LET'S EAT"
Draw 1 PROTEIN card.

PLAY WITH A FRIEND
Have twice the fun.
Draw 2 "Let's Play" cards.

VEGETABLES
"LET'S EAT"
Draw 1 VEGETABLES card.

COUCH POTATO
"LET'S EAT"
Return 1 "Let's Play" card.

UN-SATURATED FAT
"LET'S EAT"
Draw 1 Unsaturated FAT card.

"I'M HUNGRY"
Draw 1 "Let's Eat" card.

COUCH POTATO WITH A SWEET TOOTH
Return 1 "Let's Play" card and 1 "Let's Eat" card.

COMPLEX CARBOHYDRATES
"LET'S EAT"
Draw 1 Complex CARBOHYDRATE card.

LOW-FAT DAIRY
"LET'S EAT"
Draw 1 Low-Fat DAIRY card.

SWEET TOOTH
Return 1 "Let's Eat" card.

VEGE-TABLES
"LET'S EAT"
Draw 1 VEGETABLES card.

PLAY WITH A FRIEND
HAVE TWICE THE FUN
Draw 2 "Let's Play" cards.

COMPLEX CARBO-HYDRATES
"LET'S EAT"
Draw 1 Complex CARBOHYDRATE card.

COUCH POTATO
"LET'S EAT"
Return 1 "Let's Play" card.

UN-SATURATED FAT
"LET'S EAT"
Draw 1 Unsaturated FAT card.

"I'M THIRSTY"
"LET'S EAT"
Draw 1 "Let's Play" card and 1 "Let's Eat" card.

PROTEIN
"LET'S EAT"
Draw 1 PROTEIN card.

SWEET TOOTH
Return 1 "Let's Eat" card.

FRUIT
"LET'S EAT"
Draw 1 FRUIT card.

COUCH POTATO
Return 1 "Let's Play" card.

FRUIT
Draw 1 FRUIT card.

COUCH POTATO
"LET'S EAT"
Return 1 "Let's Play" card.

"I'M THIRSTY"
Draw 1 "Let's Play" card and 1 "Let's Eat" card.

THE BALANCING ACT

GAMES

1. The Balancing Act
(board game)

2. B-A-L-A-N-C-E
(card game)

3. Tossed Salad
(card game)

4. The Juggling Act
(a way to balance
your lifestyle)

1

THE BALANCING ACT

▲

A board game for 2-4 players   Ages 6 to adult

Contents

The game board (see p. 150).

104 cards (see pp. 156-69) = 16 *"Yes, I Can"* cards, 5 *Sweet Tooth* cards, 42 *"Let's Eat"* cards (7 each of PROTEIN, Complex CARBOHYDRATE, Unsaturated FAT, Low-Fat DAIRY, FRUIT, and VEGETABLES), 3 *"I'm Hungry"* cards, 6 *"I'm Thirsty"* cards, and 16 *"Let's Play"* cards.

Preparation: This fast-moving board game is designed to help you review the things you learned in Part 1 (see pp. 1-30). Putting this board game together is almost as much fun as playing it!

1. Enlarge the board 200% using a copy machine with magnification capabilities. Glue to a poster board. Color with markers.

2. Glue a 6" x 9" clasp envelope onto the inside back cover of this book to hold the cards. Photocopy the fronts of all of the cards on pp. 156-69. Glue the copies of the cards onto lightweight cardboard, such as manila folders. Color the cards with markers. Carefully cut out each card with scissors.

3. Use 2 sheets of white typing paper. On the first sheet of paper, write the words *"Let's Play"* and then draw a picture of you playing something you love to play. Include your friends in the picture, if you like. On the second sheet of paper, write the words *"Let's Eat"* and draw a picture of your kitchen. Lay each of these sheets of paper near the game board. Stack the *"Let's Play"* cards on the picture of you playing. Stack each of the six piles of *"Let's Eat"* cards on the picture of your kitchen.

4. Use coins, buttons, or markers from other board games to mark your place as you move along the spaces of the board. Make sure every player's marker is different. Keep markers in a plastic bag.

5. You can use one or two dice. Store the dice with the markers in the plastic bag.

If you do not have any dice, make *Move It* cards. Cut 36 2" x 3" rectangles from colored construction paper. Number each card with 1, 2, 3, 4, 5, or 6, until all cards are numbered. Write the words *Move It* on the backs of all the rectangles. To use cards, mix them up and turn them face down. Draw the top card and move your marker the same number of squares as the number on the card. Put the card face down under the pile of *Move It* cards. Store these cards with the other game cards in the envelope.

Playing the game: The object of the game is to get 5 *"Yes, I Can"* cards. To get a *"Yes, I Can"* card, you must match any *"Let's Play"* card and the appropriate *"Let's Eat"* card with one of the *Kids* cards.

Play this game with your family and friends. Everyone can learn that it takes both lively physical activities and nutritious foods to achieve a healthy body, and that having a positive attitude can make all the difference in your success.

1. Lay the board on a table. Place the *"Let's Play"* and *"Let's Eat"* pictures nearby and stack the appropriate cards on each picture. You can chose one person to be in charge of handing out the cards. Place the *Move It* cards where everyone can reach them. Place the *"Yes, I Can"* cards in the triangle in the center of the board. Place the markers on the Start space.

2. Deal each player 5 *Kids* cards in

a clockwise direction. Then deal each player 2 *"Let's Play"* cards. Place the remaining cards on the *"Let's Play"* picture.

3. Each player draws a card from the *Move It* pile or throws the dice. The highest number goes first. Play in a clockwise direction.

4. The first player draws a card from the *Move It* pile or throws the dice, moves the marker the same number of spaces, and follows the directions on the space.

5. The next player repeats step 4.

6. Eventually, a player will draw a *"Let's Eat"* card that matches one of the *Kids* cards. Keep the two together. When the player also draws a *"Let's Play"* card, it can be put with the other two cards. During a regular turn, these three cards can be placed in the center of the game board and traded for a *"Yes, I Can"* card and for another *Kids* card.

7. Players draw one *"Let's Play"* card when they pass Start or two if they land there. Players can use the *"Let's Play"* card as soon as they pass Start. Then they follow the directions on the space where they land.

8. When players run out of any cards to draw, they should stop long enough to return the cards from the center of the board to the appropriate pile.

9. The first player to collect 5 *"Yes, I Can"* cards first is the winner.

10. HAVE FUN!

2

B-A-L-A-N-C-E

A card game for 2-4 players   Ages 6 to adult

Playing the game: The object of the game is for a player to place in sequence each of the 7 cards listed below and spell B-A-L-A-N-C-E.

B = "Let's Play"

A = PROTEIN

L = Complex CARBOHYDRATES

A = Unsaturated FAT

N = Low-Fat DAIRY

C = FRUIT

E = VEGETABLES

1. Gather the deck: 42 *"Let's Eat"* cards; 7 *"Let's Play"* cards; 6 *Kids* cards; 5 *"Yes, I Can"* cards; and 5 *Sweet Tooth* cards. Shuffle them.

2. Deal 6 cards to each player. Place the remaining cards face down in the center of the table. Turn the top card face up next to the pile. This becomes the discard pile.

3. Play in a clockwise direction, beginning with the dealer.

4. The first player draws a card. The player may draw from either pile. The player may not, however, draw a *"Yes, I Can"* card from the discard pile.

5. After drawing a card, the player then discards one card. The player may place a card on the table, face up, or discard a card in the discard pile. The cards in front of the player must be played in sequence.

6. The second player then draws a card and discards a card as explained in steps 4 and 5 above.

7. If all the cards are drawn from the pile before play ends, shuffle the discard pile, place it face down, and turn the top card face up next to the pile.

8. Play ends when one player has placed all 7 cards in sequence on the table.

Kids card: This is a wild card. It can be used in place of any of the needed 7 cards. It can be used as many times as needed. A player simply replaces it with the necessary card during his or her regular turn, and it can be used again in the same turn. However, a player may have only one of these wild cards on the table at a time. For example, if the wild card is played for a FRUIT card, the player can replace the wild card with a FRUIT card and use the wild card for a VEGETABLES card.

"Yes, I Can" card: When you have this card, you can give it to the player of your choice during any of your turns. The player must trade his/her cards on the table with you.

Sweet Tooth card: When you draw this card, you must immediately trade your cards on the table with another player who has fewer cards on the table than you do.

3
TOSSED SALAD
▲

A card game for any number of players
Ages 6 to adult

Playing the game: The object is to match any 2 cards until all the cards are matched. The first player to score more than 20 points is the winner.

1. Gather the cards: 2 matching *"Let's Eat"* cards from each of the 6 food categories; any 4 *"Let's Play"* cards since there are no matching cards; 2 *"I'm Hungry"* cards; 2 *"I'm Thirsty"* cards, 2 *"Yes, I Can"* cards, and 2 *Sweet Tooth* cards.

2. Shuffle the cards and place them face down in random order, in 4 rows with 6 cards per row.

3. All cards must remain in the same position until they are matched with another card and removed.

4. Play in a clockwise direction, beginning with the dealer.

5. The first player turns over 2 cards so that the other players can see them clearly. Players who fail to do this will lose their turn.

6. If the cards do not match, the player turns them face down and the next player repeats step 5.

7. If the cards do match, the player takes them. This is called a set. The player repeats step 5. The player continues to take cards as long as they match.

8. When all the cards are matched, total the number of sets per person (1 point per set). Write down the totals. The first player to score more than 20 points is the winner. If two players score more than 20 points, then the highest score is the winner.

9. Shuffle the cards after each game. Deal rotates in a clockwise direction after each hand.

JARED EATS **VEGETABLES** ▲

GINGER EATS **PROTEIN** ▲

WORTH EATS **LOW-FAT DAIRY** ▲

KEVIN EATS **COMPLEX CARBOHYDRATES** ▲

ADAM EATS **UNSATURATED FAT** ▲

KELLI EATS **FRUIT** ▲

PAUL EATS **VEGETABLES** ▲

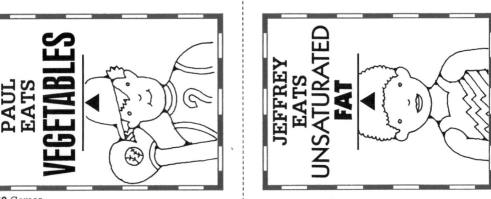

JEFFREY EATS **UNSATURATED FAT** ▲

KAYSIE EATS
LOW-FAT DAIRY ◀

AARON EATS
VEGETABLES ◀

RICKY EATS
FRUIT ◀

JAIME EATS
FRUIT ◀

MELINDA EATS
PROTEIN ◀

MATTHEW EATS
VEGETABLES ◀

ROBERT EATS
UNSATURATED FAT ◀

STEPHANIE EATS
COMPLEX CARBOHYDRATES ◀

LARRY EATS
PROTEIN
▲

ALEXANDRA EATS
FRUIT
▲

LISA EATS
LOW-FAT DAIRY
▲

DENNIS EATS
COMPLEX CARBOHYDRATES
▲

JIMMY EATS
COMPLEX CARBOHYDRATES
▲

JENNIFER EATS
PROTEIN
▲

ANGELA EATS
VEGETABLES
▲

CLINT EATS
UNSATURATED FAT
▲

"LET'S EAT"

L

COMPLEX CARBO-HYDRATES

"LET'S EAT"

A

UN-SATURATED **FAT**

"LET'S EAT"

L

COMPLEX CARBO-HYDRATES

"LET'S EAT"

L

COMPLEX CARBO-HYDRATES

"LET'S EAT"

L

COMPLEX CARBO-HYDRATES

"LET'S EAT"

L

COMPLEX CARBO-HYDRATES

"LET'S EAT"

L

COMPLEX CARBO-HYDRATES

"LET'S EAT"

L

COMPLEX CARBO-HYDRATES

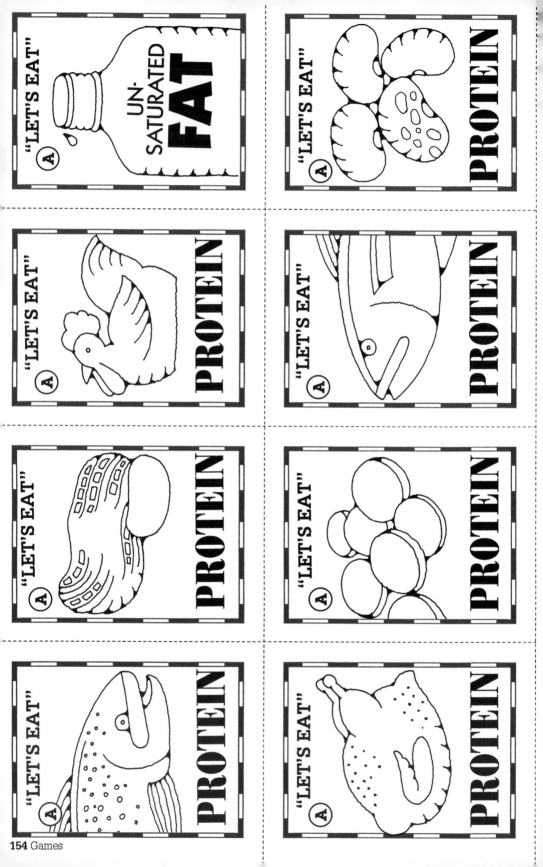

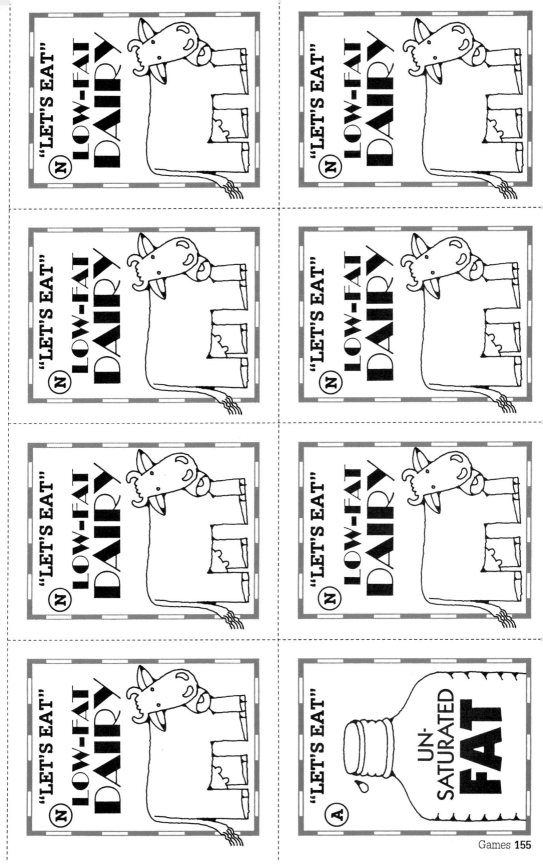

"LET'S EAT"

(C)

FRUIT

"LET'S EAT"

(C)

FRUIT

"LET'S EAT"

(C)

FRUIT

"LET'S EAT"

(C)

FRUIT

"LET'S EAT"

(A)

UN-SATURATED FAT

"LET'S EAT"

(C)

FRUIT

"LET'S EAT"

(C)

FRUIT

"LET'S EAT"

(C)

FRUIT

"LET'S EAT"
E
VEGETABLES

"LET'S EAT"
A
UN-SATURATED FAT

"LET'S EAT"
E
VEGETABLES

"LET'S EAT"
E
VEGETABLES

"LET'S EAT"
E
VEGE-TABLES

"LET'S EAT"
E
VEGETABLES

"LET'S EAT"
E
VEGETABLES

"LET'S EAT"
E
VEGETABLES

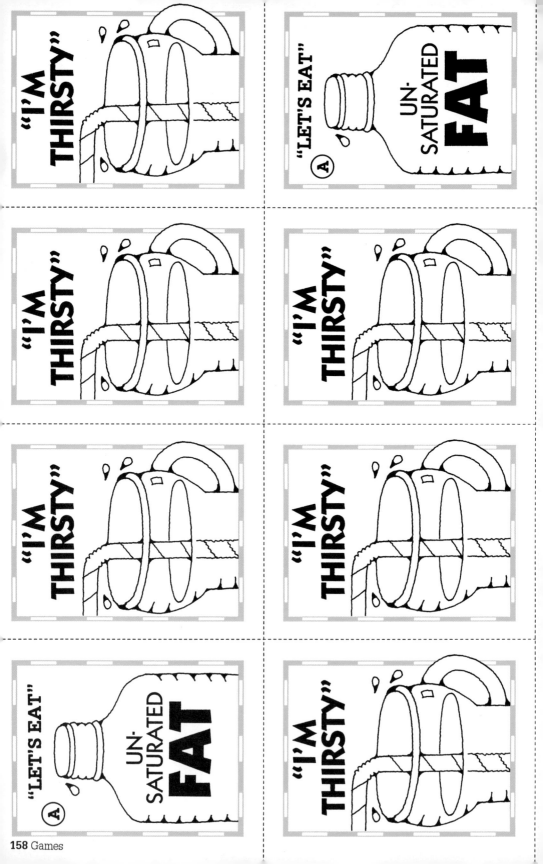

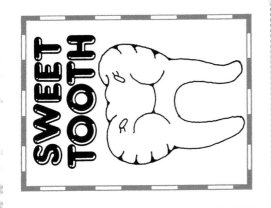

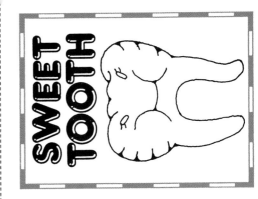

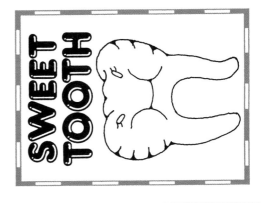

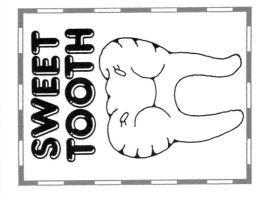

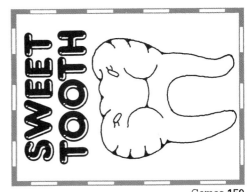

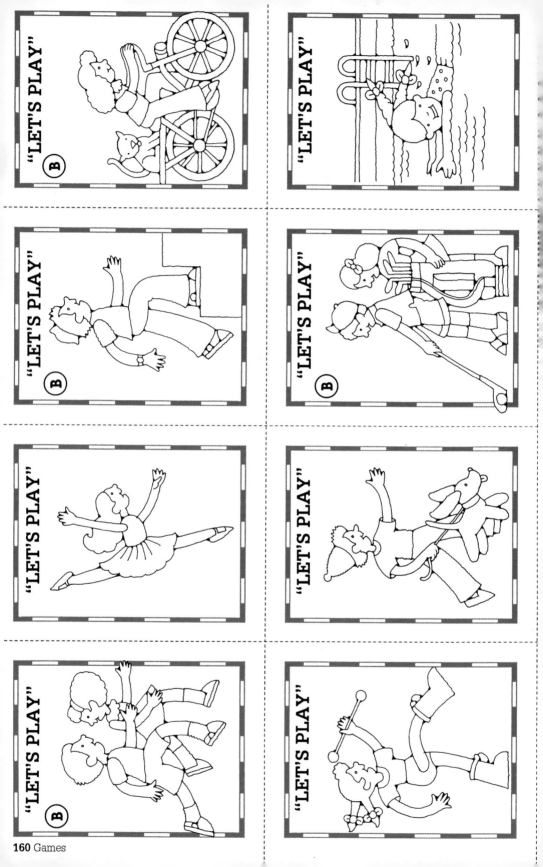

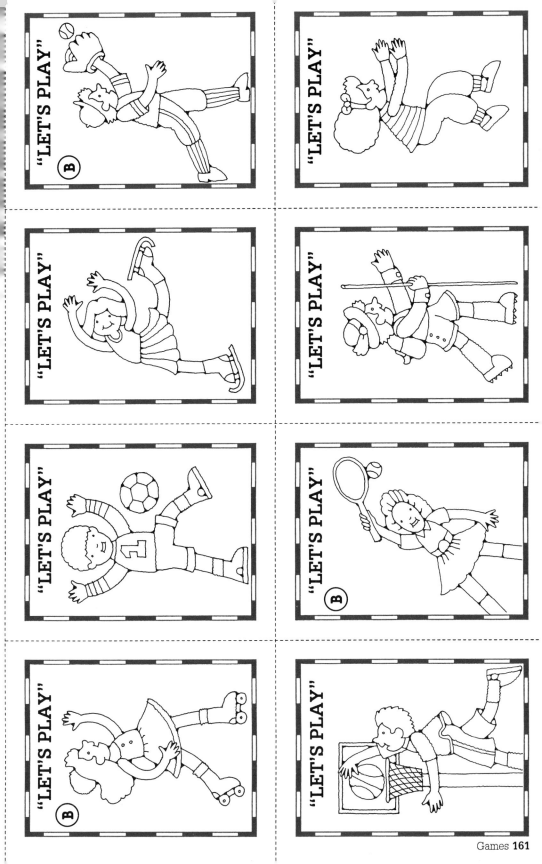

"LET'S PLAY" (B)

"LET'S PLAY"

"LET'S PLAY"

"LET'S PLAY"

"LET'S PLAY"

"LET'S PLAY" (B)

"LET'S PLAY" (B)

"LET'S PLAY"

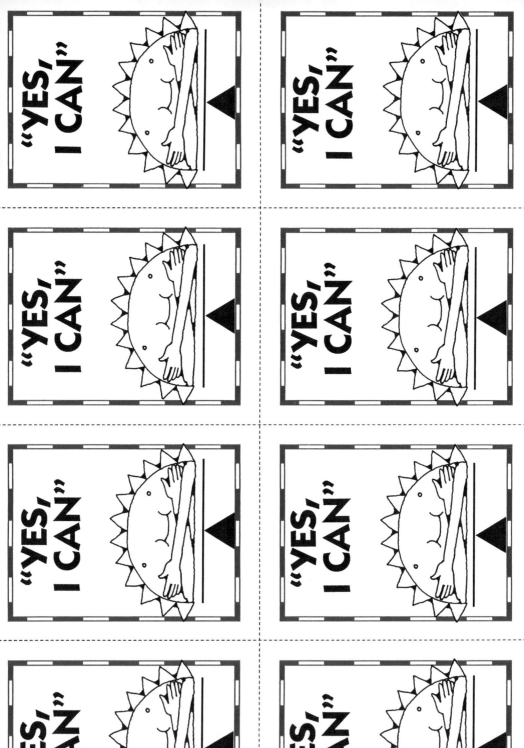

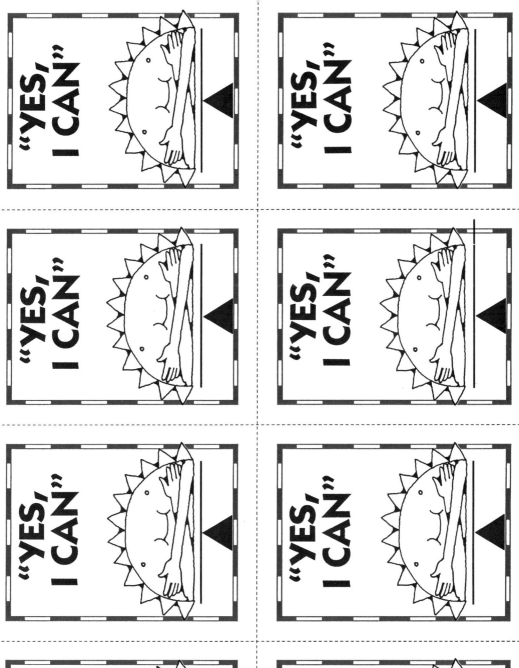

"YES, I CAN"

"YES, I CAN"

"YES, I CAN"

"YES, I CAN"

"YES, I CAN"

"YES, I CAN"

"YES, I CAN"

"YES, I CAN"

THE JUGGLING ACT

We have already learned that diets don't work (see p. 2). But keeping track of what you eat and how much you play is not a diet. It is a good way to understand your lifestyle and make adjustments if necessary.

For about two weeks, write down everything you eat, where you are when you eat, who you are with, and what time it is. Do the same thing for the times you play. This will help you see your lifestyle patterns. At the end of the two weeks, talk these lifestyle patterns over with an adult. Can you see any adjustments that need to be made? If you do, choose one area and set a goal to make that adjustment. For example, perhaps you do not eat enough vegetables. Set a goal to eat vegetables 3 times a day. Focus on your new goal for 1 month. By then it will become a habit and much easier to do. This is a good thing to do any time you feel that you are not in control of your lifestyle. (See p. 30 for more ideas.)

After a while, you will understand your lifestyle patterns enough that you will be able to track them without writing them down. You can use this wall hanging and colored cards.

1. You can make the following wall hanging with the help of an adult. Hang it in your kitchen or bedroom. You will need a 14-inch by 18-inch piece of felt and a 24-inch piece of cord. If you have pinking shears, use them to cut out the felt.

a. Cut a 2-inch strip from the bottom of the felt. Set aside.

b. On the large piece, fold the bottom up 2 inches and pin it in place. Stitch it into 6 pockets.

c. Lay the felt or fabric strip 5 inches from the bottom of the wall hanging. Stitch it into place and then into 6 pockets.

d. Using a marker, label each pocket to match the drawing on p. 165.

e. Using a marker, write *"Yes, I Can"* across the top of the wall hanging. Decorate it with a sunburst.

f. Stitch the cord to each upper corner of the wall hanging.

g. You are finished, unless you want to make it more fancy.

2. Now you are ready to make the cards. Copy a special set of cards from pp. 150-63. Color the cards with a marker. You will need:

11	**Complex CARBOHYDRATE cards (brown)**
3	**PROTEIN cards (red)**
3	**FRUIT cards (orange)**
4	**VEGETABLES cards (dark green)**
2	**Unsaturated FAT cards (yellow)**
3	**Low-Fat DAIRY cards (dark blue)**
16	*"Let's Play"* **cards (purple)**
6	*"I'm Hungry"* **cards (light green)**
6	*"I'm Thirsty"* **cards (light blue)**

7 *"Yes, I Can"* **cards (multi-colored)**

3 *Sweet Tooth* **cards (pink)**

10 **Blank rectangles cut from black construction paper**

3. Place all the cards in the upper left-hand pocket. As you go through your day, move the appropriate card from that pocket to its own pocket.

4. Each card represents:

"Let's Eat" = one food serving (see pp. 5-20.)

"Let's Play" = ten minutes of playing (see pp. 21-24.)

"I'm Hungry" = successfully eating in harmony with your hunger drives (see p. 8.)

"I'm Thirsty" = 1 glass of water. Drink about 6 glasses of water a day (see p. 9.)

Sweet Tooth = eating too much sugar (see p. 10.)

A black rectangle = an action not in keeping with a healthy lifestyle, such as eating too many grams of fat or eating when you are not hungry.

"Yes, I Can" = your reward for a good attitude (see pp. 25-30.) Pin one to your wall hanging each time you earn one during the week.

At the end of every day, you can see by the location of your cards where you have been successful. Every day is a new opportunity to control your lifestyle and to feel good about being you.

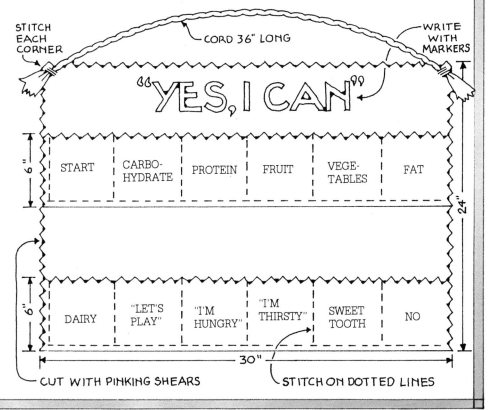

recipes for KIDS

INDEX

A

Abbreviations, 44
Adjusting recipes, 34-35
Anorexia, 135
Applesauce
    Funny-Face Sandwich, 66
    Simple Sassy Sauce, 59
    Tutti-Frutti Treat, 67

B

Baking
    Ant Hills, 54
    Bread Machines, 121
    Monkey Muffins, 55
    "No Need to Knead" Bread, 120
Bananas
    Banana Blizzard, 53
    Birthday Banana Split, 104
    Frozen Fruit Snow, 105
    Going Ape, 48
    Monkey Muffins, 55
    Up and Down the Scales, 70

Beans
    about, 15
    Geometry Chips, 71
    Hot-Shot Chili, 119
    Pita Pizza, 81
    Sombrero Salad, 117
Beef, 14-15, 34
Binges, 137
Blender
    Alaskan Sunrise, 52
    Frozen Fruit Snow, 105
    Ice Hockey, 79
Bread
    Bread Machines, 121
    Funny-Face Sandwich, 66
    I Love Pizza, 96
    "My Hero" Sandwich, 99
    "No Need to Knead" Bread, 120
    Pick Pockets, 80
    Pita Pizza, 81
    Single Simple Cinnamon French
    Toast, 57
    Whole Wheat Honey Bread, 121
Breakfast
    about, 46
    ideas, 45-60, 63
Bulimia,135
Butter, 16-19, 34

C

Calories, 18-19
Carbohydrates
    about, 6, 10-11, 19
    complex, 11
    refined, 10
    servings, 7-8
    simple, 10
    unrefined, 11
Cereal
    Airborne, 50
    "Go Get Dressed for School"
    Oatmeal, 51
    Going Ape, 48
    Snic Snac Bars, 103
    Spare Parts, 78
    Store-purchased, 50-51
    Tutti-Frutti Treat, 67
Cheese
    about, 20
    I Love Pizza, 96
    Toppings, 113
Chicken
    about, 14-15, 34
    Hen on a Nest, 97
    "My Hero" Sandwich, 99
    Picnic Chicken Sticks, 92
    Sombrero Salad, 117
    Western Hoedown Haystacks, 116
Coloring, 40-43, 144, 146-63
Cooking Secrets, 38
Cooking Terms, 42-43
Cooking Tools, 40-41
Corn
    Cowboy-Cowgirl Stir-Fry, 114
    Geometry Chips, 71
    Sombrero Salad, 117
Cottage Cheese
    Alpine Ski Slopes, 101
    Birthday Banana Split, 104
    Coney Island Cone, 74
    Dilly Dip, 85
    Tomato Torture Chamber, 86-87
Coupons to order other books, 172-78

D

Dairy
    about, 6, 20
    servings, 7-8
Desserts
    Birthday Banana Split, 104
    Frozen Fruit Snow, 105
    Fruit juice gelatin, 72-73
    Funny-Face Sandwich, 66
    Ginger Bits, 69
    Ring-Around-the-Rosy, 100
    Snic Snac Bars, 103
    Sunburst, 100
    Tic-Tac-Toe Fruit Combo, 88
    Tutti-Frutti Treat, 67
    Up and Down the Scales, 70
Diets, 2, 18-19
Dinner ideas, 109-22
Dips
    Coney Island Cone, 74
    Dilly Dip, 85
    Orange Dip, 89
Drinks
    Alaskan Sunrise, 52
    Banana Blizzard, 53
    Frozen Fruit Snow, 105
    Grape Juice Razzle Dazzle, 95
    Ice Hockey, 79
    Wacky Wassail, 108
    Winter Warm-up, 83

E

Eggs
    about, 15, 16, 20, 34
    Alaskan Sunrise, 52
    Ham and Green Eggs, 98
    Scrambled Surprise, 90
Exercise, 7, 21-24

F

Family support, 124
Fat thermostat
    about, 3, 18
    lowering, 4
Fats
    about, 6, 16-19
    adjusting recipes, 34
    burning, 18-19
    counting grams, 19
    in dairy products, 20
    replacements, 36
    saturated, 16
    servings, 7-8
    unsaturated, 17
Fats Make Me Fat!, 16-17
Foods for Energy, 10-11
Foods for Growth, 14-15
Foods for Strength, 12-13
Freezer
    Ice Hockey, 79
    Rebounds, 73
    Sunshine Pops, 82
French Toast
    Single Simple Cinnamon French Toast, 57
    Sleep-Over French Toast, 77
Frozen fruit juice concentrate
    about, 35-36
    Alaskan Sunrise, 52
    Ice Hockey, 79
    Paint Your Pancake, 58
    Simple Sassy Sauce, 59
    Sunshine Pops, 82
    Wacky Wassail, 108
Fruits (see also Applesauce, Bananas, Drinks, Frozen fruit juice concentrate)
    about, 6, 12
    Alpine Ski Slopes, 101
    Apple-Tuna Toss, 122
    Birthday Banana Split, 104
    Frozen Fruit Snow, 105
    Fruit juice gelatin, 72-73
    Funny-Face Sandwich, 66
    Happy Holiday Salad, 107
    Indian Summer, 101
    Jungle Jumble, 49
    Ring-Around-the-Rosy, 100
    School Lunch, 64-65
    servings, 7-8
    Sunburst, 100
    Tic-Tac-Toe Fruit Combo, 88
    Tutti-Frutti Treat, 67
    Up and Down the Scales, 70
    Western Hoedown Haystacks, 116

G

Games
    B-A-L-A-N-C-E (card game), 148-63
    Balancing Act, The (board game), 146-63
    Juggling Act, The (tracking your lifestyle), 164-65
    Tic-Tac-Toe Fruit Combo, 88
    Tossed Salad (card game), 149-63
Gelatin
    about, 72-73
    Boink!, 72
    Giggles, 73
    Mellow Gellow, 73
    Patchwork, 73
    Rebounds, 73
    Wiggle, Waggle, Jiggle, Jaggle, 72
    Yikes! Stripes!, 73
Grains (see Corn, Oatmeal, Rice, Whole Wheat Flour)
Gravy, 116

H

Hamburger
    ABC Spaghetti, 118
    about, 14-15
    Cowboy-Cowgirl Stir-Fry, 114
    Hot-Shot Chili, 119
    how to cook, 119
    I Love Pizza, 96
    Sombrero Salad, 117

Holidays
  Birthday, 104
  Christmas, 108
  Easter, 97
  Father's Day, 99
  Halloween, 106
  Independence Day, 102
  Mother's Day, 98
  New Year's, 95
  Thanksgiving, 107
  Valentine's Day, 96
Honey, 35
Hunger drives, 7-8

Junk Foods, 33
Kitchen Math, 44

Labels, reading, 32-33
Legumes, 15
Lifestyle, 2, 7, 164-65
Lunch ideas
  1 Potato, 2 Potato, 3 Potato, 4, 68
  Alpine Ski Slopes, 101
  Ant Hills, 54
  Apple-Tuna Toss, 122
  Birthday Banana Split, 104
  Bronco Buster Baked Potatoes, 112
  Coney Island Cone, 74
  Cowboy-Cowgirl Stir-Fry, 114
  Frozen Fruit Snow, 105
  Fruit juice gelatin, 72-73
  Funny-Face Sandwich, 66
  Happy Holiday Salad, 107
  Hot-Shot Chili, 119
  I Love Pizza, 96
  Indian Summer, 101
  Jack-O'-Lantern Soup, 106
  Monkey Muffins, 55
  "My Hero" Sandwich, 99

  "No Need to Knead" Bread, 120
  Pick Pockets, 80
  Picnic Chicken Sticks, 92
  Pita Pizza, 81
  Ring-Around-the-Rosy, 100
  Rodeo Rice, 115
  Scrambled Surprise, 90
  Skillet Skitters, 91
  Snic Snac Bars, 103
  Sombrero Salad, 117
  Sunburst, 100
  Tic-Tac-Toe Fruit Combo, 88
  Tutti-Frutti Treat, 67
  Up and Down the Scales, 70
  Western Hoedown Haystacks, 116

Measuring ingredients, 44
Meat, 14-19 (see also Chicken,
Hamburger, Protein, Tuna)
Microwave recipes
  Bronco Buster Baked Potatoes, 112
  I Love Pizza, 96
  Spare Parts, 78
  Wacky Wassail, 108
Milk
  about, 20, 34
  Alaskan Sunrise, 52
  Banana Blizzard, 53
  Frozen Fruit Snow, 105

Nutrition Chart, 32
Nuts, 15, 17
Oatmeal
  "Go Get Dressed for School"
  Oatmeal, 51
  Going Ape, 48
  Snic Snac Bars, 103
  Tutti-Frutti Treat, 67

Oven recipes
 Ant Hills, 54
 Bronco Buster Baked Potatoes, 112
 Hen on a Nest, 97
 I Love Pizza, 96
 Monkey Muffins, 55
 Picnic Chicken Sticks, 92
 Snic Snac Bars, 103

Pancake Toppings
(see Select-A-Topping)
Pancakes
 about, 35
 House Mouse Pancakes, 56
Pasta
 ABC Spaghetti, 118
 Hen on a Nest, 97
 how to cook, 118
Pita Bread
 Pick Pockets, 80
 Pita Pizza, 81
Pork, 14-19
Positive Attitude, 7, 25-30
Potatoes
 1 Potato, 2 Potato, 3 Potato, 4, 68
 Bronco Buster Baked Potatoes, 112
 Skillet Skitters, 91
Protein
 about, 6, 14-15, 19
 servings, 7-8

Raisins
 Ant Hills, 54
 Birthday Banana Split, 104
 Coney Island Cone, 74
 Funny-Face Sandwich, 66
 Indian Summer, 101
 Snic Snac Bars, 103
 Tutti-Frutti Treat, 67

Rice
 Cowboy-Cowgirl Stir-Fry, 114
 Hen on a Nest, 97
 Rodeo Rice, 115
 Western Hoedown Haystacks, 116

Safety Secrets, 39
Salad Dressings
 Dilly Dip, 85
 Low-Fat Ranch, 34
 Orange Dip, 89
Salads
 Alpine Ski Slopes, 101
 Apple-Tuna Toss, 122
 Birthday Banana Split, 104
 Coney Island Cone, 74
 Fruit juice gelatin, 72-73
 Happy Holiday Salad, 107
 Indian Summer, 101
 Pick Pockets, 80
 Ring-Around-the-Rosy, 100
 Sombrero Salad, 117
 Sunburst, 100
 Tic-Tac-Toe Fruit Combo, 88
 Tomato Torture Chamber, 86-87
 Tutti-Frutti Treat, 67
 Up and Down the Scales, 70
 Wheels, Whirls, and Curls, 84
Salt replacements, 36
Sandwiches and Sandwich Fillings
 Apple-Tuna Toss, 122
 Funny-Face Sandwich, 66
 Ham and Green Eggs, 98
 "My Hero" Sandwich, 99
 Pick Pockets, 80
 Scrambled Surprise, 90
 Sombrero Salad, 117
School Bus Breakfasts, 63
School Lunch, 64-65
Seasonings, 36
Select-A-Topping
 Jam Session, 60
 Paint Your Pancakes, 58

Simple Sassy Sauce, 59
Tutti-Frutti Treat, 67
Self-Esteem, 25-30
Serving sizes, 6-8
Snacks
    1 Potato, 2 Potato, 3 Potato, 4, 68
    After-school snacks, 66-69
    Alaskan Sunrise, 52
    Alpine Ski Slopes, 101
    Ant Hills, 54
    Bronco Buster Baked Potatoes, 112
    Coney Island Cone, 74
    Frozen Fruit Snow, 105
    Fruit juice gelatin, 72-73
    Funny-Face Sandwich, 66
    Geometry Chips, 71
    Grape Juice Razzle Dazzle, 95
    Ice Hockey, 79
    Indian Summer, 101
    Monkey Muffins, 55
    "No Need to Knead" Bread, 120
    Pick Pockets, 80
    Pita Pizza, 81
    Ring-Around-the Rosy, 100
    Rodeo Rice, 115
    Skillet Skitters, 91
    Snic Snac Bars, 103
    Spare Parts, 78
    Sunburst, 100
    Tic-Tac-Toe Fruit Combo, 88
    Tutti-Frutti Treat, 67
    Up and Down the Scales, 70
    Wacky Wassail, 108
Soups
    Hot-Shot Chili, 119
    Jack-O'-Lantern Soup, 106
    Winter Warm-up, 83
Spices, 35-36
Sugar
    about, 10
    adjusting recipes, 35
    replacements, 36
    servings, 7

T-V

Table settings, 110
Thirst, 9
Tortillas, 71, 117
Tuna
    about, 14-15, 34
    Apple-Tuna Toss, 122
Turkey, 14-15
Vegetables (see also Corn, Potatoes)
    about, 6, 13
    Cowboy-Cowgirl Stir-Fry, 114
    Foil Fireworks, 102
    Indian Summer, 101
    "My Hero" Sandwich, 99
    School Lunch, 64-65
    Sombrero Salad, 117
    Tomato Torture Chamber, 86-87
    Western Hoedown Haystacks, 116
    Wheels, Whirls, and Curls, 84
Vitamins and Minerals
    about, 12
    servings, 7-8

W-Z

Water
    about, 9
    servings, 7
Whole Wheat Flour
    Ant Hills, 54
    Bread Machines, 121
    House Mouse Pancakes, 56
    Monkey Muffins, 55
    "No Need to Knead" Bread, 120
    Whole Wheat Honey Bread, 121
Yogurt
    about, 20, 34
    Airborne, 50
    Banana Blizzard, 53
    Dilly Dip, 85
    Mellow Gellow, 73
    Orange Dip, 89
    Sunshine Pops, 82

Recipes for Kids to Lower Their Fat Thermostats®

LaRene Gaunt and Edward A. Parent, Ph.D.
Illustrated by Dick Brown

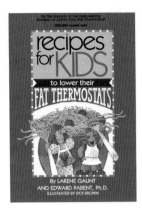

Parents and professionals agree: Diets don't work, especially for kids. Yet, little has been available to parents who want their children to eat right, look good, and be healthy—until now. *Recipes for Kids to Lower Their Fat Thermostats*, a fun, creative, full-color recipe book and guide to healthy eating, uses an interactive approach to teaching children about basic nutrition and exercise. Through activities such as coloring, games and cooking, your child will learn to choose foods that help her grow, have lots of energy, and be strong. She will learn why eating too much fat makes her fat and how to enjoy lower-fat choices. The "Tips for Mom and Dad" chapter brings you the latest research findings about childhood obesity and how you can help your child develop life-long freedom from overweight.

MasterCook II

New!
MasterCook II

MASTERCOOK II by Arion Software, makes it even easier for you to use all of your recipes. You get: A Powerful RECIPE FILER, INSTANT NUTRITIONAL ANALYSIS, and a 31-DAY MENU AND DIET PLANNER. Use your computer to help plan your meals, shopping and food budget.
• Easy to Learn, Easy to use
• Comes with over 1,000 delicious recipes including those in *Recipes to Lower Your Fat Thermostat*
• Cooking Glossary with over 500 terms
• Compatible with all major cooking programs
• Shopping List of your most frequently purchased items

MASTERCOOK makes it easier than ever to prepare delicious, wholesome meals with all your favorite recipes. Print copies of your recipes on recipe cards or in cookbook format. You can analyze your recipes using its database of over 4,500 food items. A few key strokes gives you the nutrient values of your food, including fats, cholesterol, dietary fiber, sodium and much more. Automatically finds the cost of a recipe, suggests ingredient substitutions, yields, and equivalents. You can cut, copy, and paste entire recipes. For PC Windows or Macintosh.

12 Steps To Lower Your Fat Thermostat®

Dennis Remington, M.D.; Garth Fisher, Ph.D.; Edward Parent, Ph.D.; Barbara Higa Swasey, R.D.

Have you ever felt alone in your struggle with weight control? Where do you find the daily help to be successful? *12 Steps to Lower Your Fat Thermostat* is the answer. Distilled from years of personal visits and seminars with people like you, this audiotape program works. You'll feel like you're having a private consultation with Dr. Remington, Dr. Fisher, Dr. Parent, or Barbara Higa Swasey. You'll hear each of them in person on every tape. You can listen to each step for as many times as you want. Knowledge and personal involvement are the most powerful agents for permanent change. The workbook is crammed full of information. By doing the activities suggested you'll be lowering your Fat Thermostat for comfortable, lifelong weight control.

The New Neuropsychology Of Weight Control® (Audio)

Dennis Remington, M.D.; A. Garth Fisher, Ph.D.; Edward A. Parent, Ph.D.; Barbara Higa, R.D.

More than a million people have purchased the most powerfully effective weight control program ever developed—thousands of them have reported dramatic and permanent reductions in their weight.

This Program shows you what to do to change from a fat-storing to a fat-burning metabolism. Still included are the proven principles from the original program based on the best-selling book *How to Lower Your Fat Thermostat*. Included is a complete 12-week eating plan that provides daily menus, meal plans, recipes, cooking instructions, and eight shopping lists. You'll learn to create your own delicious meals while helping you lose weight permanently.

How To Lower Your Fat Thermostat®

Dennis Remington, M.D.; A. Garth Fisher, Ph.D., Edward A. Parent; Ph.D.

Diets don't work and you know it! The less you eat, the more your body clings to its fat stores. This best-selling book contains the original program that teaches you to lose weight by giving yourself plenty of nutrients to convince the control centers in your brain to release excess fat stores. Your weight will come down naturally and comfortably, and stay at that lower level permanently.

Recipes To Lower Your Fat Thermostat®

LaRene Gaunt

Second Edition NEW for the 1990's

Companion cookbook to *How To Lower Your Fat Thermostat* and *The New Neuropsychology of Weight Control*. Now you can put principles of the Fat Thermostat program to work in your daily diet with this beautifully illustrated cookbook. It contains over 400 of your favorite recipes, a 14-day menu plan, and 16 full-color pictures. You'll find breakfast ideas, soups and salads, meats and vegetables, wok food, potatoes, beans, breads, desserts and treats. All are designed to please and satisfy while lowering your fat thermostat.

Acrylic Cookbook Holder

This acrylic cookbook holder is the perfect companion to your new cookbook. Designed to hold any cookbook open without breaking the binding, it allows you to read recipes without distortion while protecting pages from splashes and spills.

Desserts to Lower Your Fat Thermostat®

Barbara Higa, R.D.

If you think you have to say goodbye to desserts, think again. At last there's a book that lets you have your cake and eat it, too. *Desserts to Lower Your Fat Thermostat* is filled with what you thought you could never find: recipes for delicious desserts, snacks, and treats that are low in fat and free of sugar, salt, and artificial sweeteners. The 200 delectable ideas packed between the covers of this book meet the guidelines of both the American Heart Association and the American Diabetes Association. They will meet your own tough standards, too -- especially if you've been longing for winning ideas that will delight your family without destroying their health.

Back to Health:

A Comprehensive Medical and Nutritional Yeast-Control Program

Dennis Remington, M.D.; and Barbara Higa, R.D.

UPDATED FOR THE 1990's WITH AN EXPANDED PHYSICIAN SECTION

If you suffer from anxiety, depression, memory loss, heartburn, or gas . . . if weight control is a constant battle . . . if you are tired, weak, and sore all over . . . this book was written for you. While yeast occurs naturally in the body, when out of control it becomes the body's enemy, manifesting itself in dozens of symptoms. Getting yeast back under control can correct many conditions once considered chronic. More than 100 yeast-free recipes, plus special sections on weight control, hypoglycemia, and PMS.

Pocket Progress Guide

A pocket-sized summary of the Fat Thermostat program that includes food composition tables, daily records, and a program summary for quick and easy reference and record-keeping anytime, anywhere.

Easy Gourmet Menus To Lower Your Fat Thermostat®

Chef Howard Gifford

Feeling deprived? Has your diet become boring? Do you crave those wonderful foods you used to eat? Then you'll love *Easy Gourmet Menus to Lower Your Fat Thermostat*. TV's Chef Howard Gifford makes preparing healthy meals fun and exciting. Create everything from Crispy Fried Chicken to Razzleberry Cheesecake and enjoy to your heart's content. Over 150 low-fat, high-nutrition, irresistible recipes with shopping lists.

Gifford's Gourmet De-Lites

Chef Howard Gifford

You'll exclaim "This can't be low-fat! It tastes too good!" Professional Chef Howard Gifford's meals have astonished guests at weight loss health resorts, students at his Cooking school, and television viewers. *Gifford's Gourmet De-Lites* has two weeks of breakfast, lunch, and dinner menus with complete shopping lists. The recipes are a breeze to prepare. Learn how to organize your kitchen and time for the long-term solution to your weight loss questions.

The Health Deck

Chef Howard Gifford

Deal yourself a complete breakfast, lunch, dinner, and dessert. The Health Deck is perfect for those on the run who demand excellence in the food they eat. It has 52 vibrantly full-colored cards and over 175 low-fat, great tasting recipes. You also get an 80-minute cooking tips video, a 48-page Achieving Success manual, and an instant recipe finder computer program. Each card has shopping lists for 1, 2 or 4 people, so it is ideal for today's smaller sized families.

Gifford's Spice Mixes

Chef Howard Gifford has just made your cooking easier. Now the unique flavors created by Chef Gifford can be had at the shake of a bottle. Eliminate the cupboard full of spices that are seldom used and the time of mixing and measuring spices. No more guess-work to create a desired taste. These new spice mixes are conveniently packaged with six inviting flavors. Use these spice mixes with the delicious recipes in *Recipes to Lower Your Fat Thermostat, 2nd Edition; Easy Gourmet Menus to Lower Your Fat Thermostat* and *Gifford's Gourmet De-Lites*, or flavor your own meals with the desired spice mix. You'll be delighted by the results.

Maintaining the Miracle:
An Owner's Manual for the Human Body
Ted Adams, Ph.D.; A. Garth Fisher, Ph.D.; Frank G. Yanowitz, M.D.

Unlike most health books that teach you how to treat a problem, *Maintaining the Miracle* addresses the kind of bodily upkeep necessary to head off problems. By following the daily, monthly, and periodic suggestions for your age group you will enjoy years of trouble-free living. This is the owner's manual that should have come with your body.

Five Roadblocks to Weight Loss (Audiocassette)
Dennis Remington, M.D.; and Edward Parent, Ph.D.

If you have a serious weight problem that has resisted your best efforts, you could be suffering from any of the five roadblocks to weight loss: food addictions, artificial sweeteners, food allergies, yeast overgrowth, and stress. Learn what these roadblocks are and what to do about them...in an exclusive interview with Drs. Dennis Remington and Edward Parent.

QTY	CODE	DESCRIPTION	RETAIL	SUBTOTAL
	A	How to Lower Your Fat Thermostat	$9.95	
	B	Recipes to Lower Your Fat Thermostat#	$15.95	
	C	Acrylic Cookbook Holder	$9.95	
	D	New Neuropsychology of Weight Control (8 cassettes & guide)*	$79.95	
	E	Back to Health (Yeast/Candida Guide)	$10.95	
	F	Maintaining the Miracle	$16.95	
	H	Five Roadblocks to Weight Loss (Audiocassette)	$7.95	
	I	Pocket Progress Guide	$2.95	
	K	Recipes for Kids to Lower Their Fat Thermostats	$15.95	
	M	MasterCook II (Computer Recipe and Nutrition Program)@	$39.95	
	N	Desserts to Lower Your Fat Thermostat	$12.95	
	O	Gifford's Gourmet De-Lites#	$12.95	
	P	Easy Gourmet Menus to Lower Your Fat Thermostat#	$13.95	
	Q	Chef Howard Gifford's Health Deck	$59.95	
	R	Chef Howard Gifford's Menu of the Month Cards (6 cards)+	$14.95	
	S	Gifford's Gourmet De-Lites Spice Mix Set (6 bottles)#	$18.95	
	S3	Individual Spices - Basic (SB), Chinese (SC), Dessert (SD), Gourmet (SG), Italian (SI), Mexican (SM) — Circle the spice of your choice (three 2 oz. containers of same spice per package).	$9.95	
	T	12 Steps to Lower Your Fat Thermostat (6 cassettes, workbook)*	$79.95	
		Shipping & Handling, $2.50 for the 1st item, $.50 each additional item.	+	
		Canadian: $6.00 (U.S. dollars) for 1st item, $2.00 each additional item.	+	
		For faster delivery, usually under five days, by UPS, add $1.50.(Excludes Alaska & Hawaii)	+	
		* Buy D or T and get 1 book free! Utah residents add 6.25% sales tax.	+	
		# Buy B, O, or P, and receive $5.00 off for item S. @ Buy M and receive $10.00 off another item. + Buy any Gifford product and recieve R for $5.95. (Limited to product on hand.) TOTAL		

Prices subject to change without notice

Name_____DayPhone_____

Address_____

City_____State_____Zip_____

☐ Check   ☐ Money Order - Make payable to: Vitality House Publishing
☐ MasterCard   ☐ VISA   ☐ American Express   ☐ Discover Card

Card Number_____Expiration_____

Signature_____

How did you hear about our products? ☐ Friend   ☐ Book   ☐ Other _____

Mail to: Vitality House Publishing, 1675 No. Freedom Blvd. #11-C, Provo, UT 84604-2570 (801)373-5100
Copyright© 1994 Vitality House International, Inc. Orders shipped upon receipt. Allow 2-3 weeks shipping.
TO ORDER CALL TOLL FREE: 1-800-748-5100
OR FAX YOUR ORDER TO: 801-373-5370
RFK694